MW01048949

The Greenhouse Book

Tom Brown

The Greenhouse Book

Make the most of your greenhouse throughout the year

Contents

A greenhouse can be a place to lose yourself in the gentle pleasure of tending plants.

Introduction

A greenhouse of any size, shape, or form can be game-changer when it comes to the plants you can grow. Not only do they allow you to extend the growing season and tailor the conditions to suit specific plants, but they can also transform your experience as a gardener. Nurturing plants under glass from seed to spectacular specimen can help you flourish as much as your plants.

I'm lucky enough to have a couple greenhouses at home, and as part of my job as Head Gardener at West Dean Gardens in West Sussex in the UK, I am responsible for 13 large Victorian glasshouses and a plant collection that includes tropical plants, ferns, orchids, cacti, apricots, peaches, nectarines, figs, and kiwis, as well as eggplants, cucumbers, tomatoes, peppers, and chilies.

Growing plants in my own greenhouses at home in particular has given me a great deal of joy and an enhanced sense of well-being. The pleasure that comes from growing your own plants under glass is limitless. Nurturing seedlings through every stage of their development to the point where you're harvesting food or flowers gives great satisfaction, and those fruits and vegetables taste all the more delicious when you know you have lovingly tended them yourself from seed to plate.

There is plenty to learn along the way. Greenhouse growing is an intense way to garden; plants need water, nutrients, and specific conditions and suffer far more rapidly than they do in a garden. Part of managing a greenhouse is heightening your sensitivity to the plants' needs and then modestly changing the conditions for optimum growth. It's worth mentioning, however, that when creating the right environment for the plants you choose to grow, you are also creating the perfect environment for you. Like my greenhouses at home, your greenhouse space is yours and yours alone. Make it your sanctuary, a place where you can listen to the radio or podcasts while you tend to your plants or simply spend time relaxing, surrounded by foliage, flowers, and fruit. This simple pleasure offers a huge amount of escapism from the everyday stresses of life—a testament to this is how quickly time rushes by when you are working to your own agenda and at your own pace in your greenhouse. Many a time I've been caught out, having spent hours tinkering with my plants, unaware of the time passing. And I wouldn't have it any other way.

BIGGER

Every inch of a greenhouse can be used for growing plants, from floor to ceiling.

A greenhouse for all seasons

I hope this book will inspire gardeners to make the most of their greenhouses–and not just in the summer months. These structures shouldn't become dumping grounds or storage facilities in the winter; the potential for you to grow plants in them at this time of year, or to overwinter plants in them, is far too great to ignore. Not only should we be making the most of every season in our greenhouse to produce food, grow flowers, and offer extra protection to certain plants, but we should also be making use of every possible space within the greenhouse. Hanging baskets full of herbs and strawberries can inhabit the roof space, for example, maximizing the growing potential of your greenhouse, regardless of its scale.

There is a world of crops and plants that we can cultivate in greenhouses, but like many forms of gardening, it's best to start slowly, gain experience and confidence, and then expand your repertoire as your greenhouse-growing instincts develop. The last thing I want is for you to lose confidence by trying to do too much in the first year. There will be successes and some failures, but as time goes by and you learn to read your plants, a whole range of possibilities for more challenging crops and plants will open up to you.

Your greenhouse guide

This book will take you on your greenhouse growing journey from start to finish. We'll cover choosing and building your greenhouse, whether it's brand new or second-hand. And once you have your structure up and running, there will be plenty of advice and guidance about essential growing techniques, as well as lots of ideas about what plants to grow and when through plant profiles, sowing calendars, and seasonal jobs.

Greenhouses come in all shapes and sizes–they can range from enormous structures, all the way down to a cold frame or cloche–so there's an option to suit everyone, whatever their outdoor space. As part of this book, I have grown plants in a large greenhouse, a small greenhouse, an even smaller lean-to greenhouse, and a free-standing glass cold frame to acclimatize young plants to the outdoor conditions. Each and every one of these growing environments has the potential for you to cultivate an exciting range of plants that you can have fun with.

I wish you every success and happiness with your greenhouse growing and hope you get as much joy from it as I do. Remember, the most important thing is to enjoy your greenhouse as a space that not only nurtures your plants, but nurtures you, too.

Choosing and building

Why grow under glass?

If you're undecided whether growing plants in a greenhouse or a cold frame is for you, then I would wholeheartedly say that there's a huge amount of pleasure, understanding, and satisfaction that can be had from raising plants under glass.

Watching plants grow from seeds and cuttings, and extending the season during which they flower or produce food, is a joy that I find never wanes.

Offering protection

The term "growing under glass" can mean looking after plants in a greenhouse environment, in a cold frame, or even simply under a cloche or on a windowsill. In doing so, we are controlling some of those environmental factors, such as heat, humidity, food, light, and water, that can help plants grow strongly, offering a more optimum microclimate compared to less favorable conditions outside. Growing plants in a protected environment can also help extend the growing season. Warmer ambient temperatures under glass in the early spring and late fall mean that plants will continue to grow strongly, whereas outside they would slow right down or stop entirely. For example, early salads can be harvested much sooner under glass, while tomatoes will continue to ripen in early fall due to the protected microclimate of a greenhouse. Terms like "microclimate" may seem awfully grand, but they are as relevant to a mini greenhouse or cold frame as to a larger structure. Three main structures constitute growing under glass: greenhouses, cold frames, and cloches.

Greenhouses

These are structures with a roof and sides mainly or entirely clad in a transparent material, such as glass or plastic. Greenhouses can be freestanding or supported against a building (see page 16), large or small, but all offer a warmer environment for plants to grow strongly, often with increased light and heat.

Cold frames

Often lying flat on the ground, cold frames are shallow structures with transparent roofs or lids that are usually hinged so they can be propped open and closed again (see page 24). Cold frames

A greenhouse greatly expands the range of plants that can be grown in a garden.

Space-saving options for smaller gardens and patios include miniature "lean-to" greenhouses.

offer plants protection from cold and adverse weather and are used especially for acclimatizing young plants to the outdoor environment.

Cloches

Cloches are small, portable structures made of glass or rigid plastic (see page 30). Designed to protect small groups or individual plants from wet and cold, they also offer protection from pests, especially for vulnerable seedlings or young plants.

Part of a process

All three structures can be used in conjunction to prepare plants for growing on in the open garden. Seeds germinate and young plants sprout in the warmth of a greenhouse, followed by "hardening off" in a cold frame from exposure to progressively tougher conditions. Once plants are in the soil, cloches provide temporary relief from cold nights without having to disturb the establishing roots.

Cold frames (top) can have single or double (as here) angled roofs.

Cloches (above) are especially useful for protecting new plants against unexpected late frosts.

A potted history of greenhouses

Humanity has been managing growing environments since at least Roman times, when references to covered systems first appear. Although many practices have changed, it's heartening to think that we have been using our instincts and manipulating conditions to grow healthy plants for thousands of years, resulting in one of the gardener's most indispensable innovations: the greenhouse.

Greenhouse gardening really started to take off during the17th century due to the aristocratic obsession with growing orange trees. Native to China, the orange tree had been introduced to Europe toward the end of the13th century and cemented itself as a symbol of wealth and status. This obsession for growing oranges spread north to the UK, and the desire to grow these tender plants led to the erection of sheds around the trees to protect them from the harsh winter weather. The reality was that, with no glass in the shed structure to allow light to penetrate during the winter, the orange trees were more likely to die from a lack of light and the fumes from the heaters than the cold.

The Orangery at Kensington Palace in London was built in 1704 at Queen Anne's request to house her prized orange trees during winter.

The roots of orangeries

The poor results from using these sheds, and the sheer amount of work that was required to dismantle and re-erect them every year, soon encouraged architects in the first half of the 18th century to build large, glass-roofed, decorative orangeries. These grand buildings were often very elaborate and used for great social occasions, with the orange trees often being slightly sidelined by the social event, but they did allow gardeners to overwinter their orange trees and then place them in the garden for the summer. Eventually, growing oranges became less fashionable, and rarer, more exotic plants took their place. The dramatic *Monstera deliciosa*, for example, became more desirable with its lush foliage, which screamed of tropical, distant climes. Although the concept of the greenhouse had begun in 17th-century Europe, particularly the

The Palm House at the Royal Botanic Gardens, Kew was built between 1844 and 1848 on an unprecedented scale.

Netherlands and the UK, they were soon springing up across the Atlantic. Andrew Faneuil, a wealthy merchant from Boston, built the first American greenhouse in 1737.

The grand greenhouse

As the need for increased light levels in which to grow tropical plants became apparent, additional glass was added to the roof of the orangery structure, marking their evolution to plant or forcing houses. Improvements in the manufacturing of glass then sparked the transition from architect-led orangeries to collaborations with engineers to build more recognizable greenhouses.

The marriage of more cheaply manufactured iron and the production of high-quality glass led to the construction of the first iron and glass plant house, built at Wollaton Hall just outside Nottingham in 1823. Similar large structures soon followed, such as the Great Conservatory at Chatsworth House in Derbyshire—with its framework of wood supported by iron columns—completed in 1840, and the vast iron-framed Palm House at the Royal Botanic Gardens at Kew, begun in 1844. Following the abolition of the glass tax, the development of cast plate glass, and renowned garden designer Joseph Paxton's magnificent design of the Crystal Palace for the Great Exhibition of 1851, hugely ambitious greenhouses were now the order of the day.

The Victorian era heralded the golden years of greenhouse growing with the rapid development of large greenhouses, tapping into the aristocratic need to outdo their peers with increasingly larger and more elaborate structures. Commercial-scale greenhouses, however, did not become common until the 20th century, originating in the Netherlands, predominantly to grow vines, fruits, and vegetables.

The domestic greenhouse

The aristocratic fashion for growing exotic fruits and flowers out of season soon trickled down through the social classes, with greenhouses becoming smaller and more proportionate to the average plot to fit into domestic gardens. Today, most greenhouse gardeners use their structures to grow a range of plants for food and for ornamental purposes. In many ways, our present-day ambitions to grow more of our own food at home and be mindful of its provenance echo those of the upper classes in Victorian Britain, though on a much more modest scale and with environmental concerns at the fore. The intimate relationship we form with the plants in our greenhouse is hugely rewarding, as we connect with nature on a deep level. Whether that greenhouse is large or small, the process of nurturing plants to eat or boost our well-being in these much-loved structures is here to stay.

Options for full-size greenhouses

When choosing a greenhouse for your garden, the most important considerations are the practicalities of your site, your budget, your aesthetic, and your gardening needs. There are plenty of options available for all tastes.

Metal-framed, freestanding structures are budget-friendly and can be self-assembled.

Most greenhouses have a very simple design: a freestanding structure with four sides and a peaked roof, though they can also be attached to a building. They can be built from various materials, the most common being aluminum or wood (both of which have their advantages and disadvantages; see table opposite), and can range considerably in both size and price. The glazing material can also vary from glass to polycarbonate, acrylic, or even fiberglass. You can buy greenhouses as prefabricated kits for self-assembly or employ professionals to construct them. You can even recycle second-hand ones. With such a range on offer, you're bound to find the right option for your garden and circumstances.

Choosing your material

The decision over whether to choose a wooden- or metal-framed greenhouse can be boiled down to practicality versus aesthetics. Wood is a beautiful material for a greenhouse frame, but it isn't without its drawbacks, often proving expensive and needing regular maintenance to keep it in good condition.

An aluminum frame will be low maintenance and solid enough to support polycarbonate or glass panels. Both materials can be painted in a range of colors to suit your tastes. Ultimately, budget will be key, but also think about what function your greenhouse will fulfill for you and how much of a feature it will be in your garden. To help you decide, below are a few pros and cons of each material:

Timber- or metal-framed?

	Timber	Metal
Advantages	Visually appealing with a more natural look, in keeping with a garden. The heavy frame makes the greenhouse sturdier in strong winds. Better insulated, providing more consistent temperatures. Custom and high-end appearance. More flexible design options.	Rust and rot resistant. More affordable choices available. More greenhouse for your money. Lightweight and easy to assemble. More diversity in style and options. If cared for, the frame can last for many years and can be dismantled and re-erected if moving or selling.
Disadvantages	More expensive. Heavy timber can be problematic to assemble without professional help. Higher maintenance is required, such as painting and preserving wood. Despite routine maintenance, timber will deteriorate over time. Pest build-up can be an issue, requiring more intricate cleaning.	Less insulation capability, making for more erratic temperatures. Lighter and therefore not as resilient in strong winds. Functional, less attractive appearance. Finding replacement parts can be difficult with older, second-hand models. May require strong foundations.

The greenhouse I've opted for is made of coated aluminum, giving me a large space for my budget, while the coated metal is more aesthetically sympathetic to my garden than uncoated aluminum.

Like me, I'm sure that once you've made your considered choice, you'll love your greenhouse and have endless fun in it growing a wonderful range of food and flowers.

Freestanding greenhouses

There are a wide range of styles and sizes of freestanding greenhouse to suit most tastes. This type of structure also comes in lots of different materials, making it the most popular choice. Without the need for a wall or adjoining structure to support it, a freestanding greenhouse offers us great flexibility in terms of its placement in the garden, as long as a few golden rules are adhered to (see page 36). There are plenty of second-hand options available, too, making this kind of structure affordable for most budgets (see opposite).

Lean-to greenhouses

Large attached or lean-to greenhouses work well if you have a wall available to provide the fourth side of the structure. That wall may be part of your house, an outbuilding, or a garage and is best situated on the south side of the building. This position will not only provide an opportunity to grow fan-trained fruit trees (see page 182) and climbing plants, due to the large wall space to attach training wires to, but also better heat retention and insulation than a freestanding structure.

A large, walk-in greenhouse offers great accessibility from your home, regardless of the weather. As it is attached to a building, hooking up utilities such as water, light, and heat is much easier compared to a freestanding greenhouse. This type of greenhouse tends be tailor-made to suit your building and the supporting wall, making it a more expensive option, with fewer second-hand options. Building regulations can be more problematic with larger lean-to greenhouses, as can the potential mess created by bringing compost, water, and general gardening debris closer to your home.

Large lean-tos will retain heat from the supporting wall.

Buying options

Greenhouses are most commonly bought as prefabricated kits. Prices vary considerably, and you can either assemble these kits yourself or—at an extra cost—hire a professional to build it for you. There are advantages to both these options (see page 40). Choosing a custom design constructed by building contractors is of course the most expensive, high-end option, but the results will undoubtedly be beautiful. If you're on a low budget and sustainability is an important consideration for you, however, you might want to consider buying a greenhouse second-hand.

Second-hand greenhouses

The online community of gardeners is vast, and one of the many benefits of this is the buying and selling second-hand greenhouses. Like many absorbing hobbies, growing under glass becomes addictive, and many gardeners soon realize that their original greenhouse has become too small for their needs. This appetite for more space will often result in selling their smaller greenhouse online or through a local advertisement, providing a very affordable second-hand structure for those looking to start their greenhouse journey.

When buying a used greenhouse, ensure that the frame is in good condition, without cracks or rust. A framework that is deteriorating will have a shorter lifespan, and it will end up costing you money to replace any damaged parts. Replacement glass is easy to obtain through a local glass merchant, but the higher percentage of glass that you can retain from the used greenhouse, the better. In many cases, you will need to dismantle the greenhouse at the previous owner's house, which gives you great insight into how to erect it when you get home (see page 42).

You can expect to pay a fraction of the cost of a new greenhouse, often less than 50 percent of the retail price, depending on whether or not you are required to dismantle it, but shop around to make sure you are getting the best value for money.

Wooden-framed structures are both stylish and sturdy.

Anatomy of a greenhouse

In essence, a greenhouse is a structure with roof and sides through which light can transmit. However, numerous other elements can be added to enhance further the growth of your plants.

The art of greenhouse growing is being sensitive to your plant's needs. Is your greenhouse too cold or too warm? Is the air too dry or too humid?

Optimum growth will depend on the correct amount of water, heat, and light that you provide for your plants. There are a number of functional elements that we can incorporate into the anatomy of our greenhouses–such as ventilation, shading, water harvesting, partitioning, and heating–that will help us gently manipulate the environment and create the perfect growing conditions.

Shading blinds or paint protect against strong sunlight, reducing leaf scorch and high temperatures.

Staging and shelves provide growing space for seedlings, cuttings, and small plants at a comfortable height; consider your own ergonomics to determine the ultimate height.

Hanging-basket brackets open up the roof space for growing plants such as strawberries, tomatoes, herbs, and fuchsias.

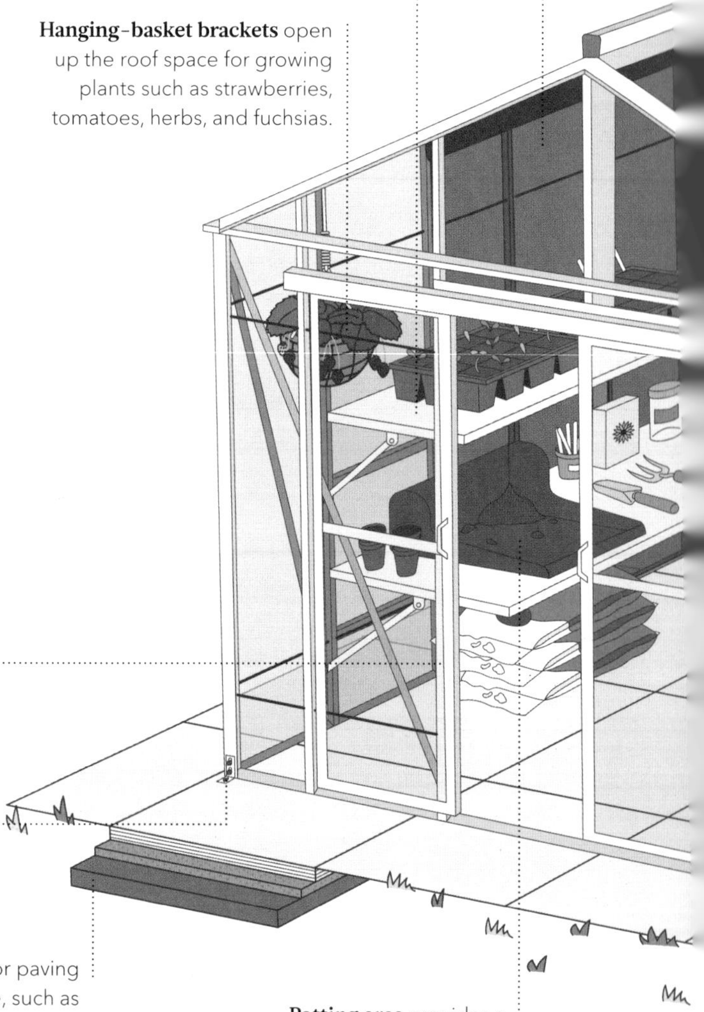

Door openings may be single or double, depending on greenhouse size and amount of access required; they provide good ventilation in summer, but can be a source of damaging cold drafts in winter.

Anchor points secure the greenhouse frame to the base or soil.

Base foundation layers suitable for paving slabs comprise a 4in (10cm) subbase, such as crushed stone, topped with 1 part cement to 6 parts sharp sand at around 2in (5cm) deep to bed in the slabs and achieve a level surface.

Potting area provides a workspace within the house to sow seeds, take cuttings, and pot on.

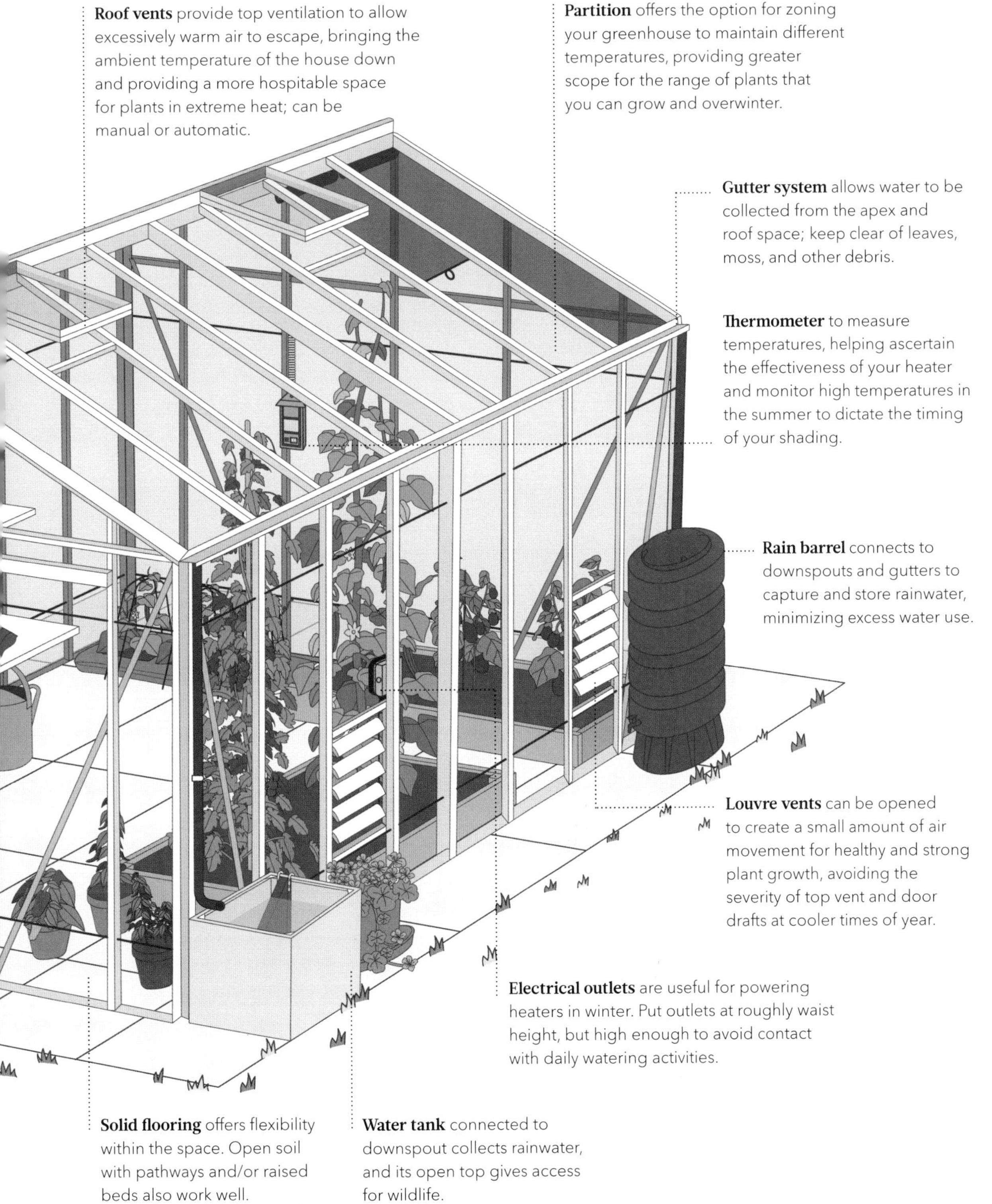

Roof vents provide top ventilation to allow excessively warm air to escape, bringing the ambient temperature of the house down and providing a more hospitable space for plants in extreme heat; can be manual or automatic.
Partition offers the option for zoning your greenhouse to maintain different temperatures, providing greater scope for the range of plants that you can grow and overwinter.
Gutter system allows water to be collected from the apex and roof space; keep clear of leaves, moss, and other debris.
Thermometer to measure temperatures, helping ascertain the effectiveness of your heater and monitor high temperatures in the summer to dictate the timing of your shading.
Rain barrel connects to downspouts and gutters to capture and store rainwater, minimizing excess water use.
Louvre vents can be opened to create a small amount of air movement for healthy and strong plant growth, avoiding the severity of top vent and door drafts at cooler times of year.
Electrical outlets are useful for powering heaters in winter. Put outlets at roughly waist height, but high enough to avoid contact with daily watering activities.
Solid flooring offers flexibility within the space. Open soil with pathways and/or raised beds also work well.
Water tank connected to downspout collects rainwater, and its open top gives access for wildlife.

Options for miniature greenhouses

You may think that to grow plants in a greenhouse you need a large garden, as the image we often have is of a free-standing structure on a patio base, but mini-greenhouses are a versatile option if you have limited space. Yes, you must be selective in the plants you grow, but the joy and experience is not diminished—it's not the size of your greenhouse but what you do with it that counts!

A smaller structure will still offer protection from the winter elements to grow hardier salads, herbs, and cut flowers during the winter and provide a more intense growing environment for summer crops, such as tomatoes and chilies. If you're new to greenhouse growing and wish to dip your toe in before investing in a more substantial greenhouse, these miniature options are a perfect way to begin.

Mini lean-to greenhouses

If you have a limited amount of space, maybe in a more urban setting, or you share the garden with soccer-loving children, a tall, slim greenhouse set against a wall—which makes use of vertical space while requiring only a small floor area—could be ideal. These structures can be clad in glass or plastic and generally, the more you invest, the more secure, robust, and long-lasting they are.

To get the best results, place them by a south-facing, sunny wall, unless you wish to grow plants such as auriculas or ferns, which would prefer less intense light and heat. Accessibility is key, so try to place your greenhouse near a door or in a space you frequently walk past to ensure that you can keep an eye on ventilation and watering needs.

Lean-tos are versatile spaces and can be adapted to grow lots of different plants at various times of the year. Shelving is particularly useful when growing seedlings and young plants in the early spring and when overwintering plants. But then, when plants dry out more quickly during the summer, small pots and trays can be time-consuming and problematic. By removing the shelves and placing a large pot or grow bag at the base, we can then adapt these miniature greenhouses to grow a variety of taller summer crops, such as tomatoes, chilies, peppers, eggplants, and cucumbers.

Sun-loving succulents, such as aeoniums, will be happy in a south-facing lean-to over the colder months and can remain on display, too.

DIY mini-greenhouses

New glass can be expensive, so to save money and be more sustainable, making a small greenhouse out of recycled materials—in particular, old windows—can be lots of fun and give you a unique structure to suit your needs and garden.

Alternatively, a large glass cloche would be perfectly adequate for raising seedlings and cuttings, as well as cultivating summer crops, such as peppers and chilies. Dwarf varieties are best suited to these mini-greenhouses, but if the plants outgrow the space, the risk of damage from the cold would have passed by the time they reach that size.

This type of greenhouse can have more height than a cold frame and has the look and feel of a "standard" greenhouse. Ventilation is key, and easy access to your plants is a must. Ensure, too, that the structure allows as much light transmission as possible for optimum plant growth.

Mini-greenhouses offer various growing options, such as (clockwise from above) large cloches for summer crops and lean-tos either without shelving for tall plants like tomatoes or with shelving for trays of seedlings.

Cold frames

Cold frames are an extremely useful addition to a greenhouse setup, offering extra space to grow seeds and to acclimatize plants. Ideally south-facing, these easy-to-build structures can extend your growing season by protecting small plants from cold and wet weather.

Cold frames as part of your greenhouse growing system offer that transitional bridge from the greenhouse to the garden by allowing you to harden off and acclimatize plants to the harsher conditions outside, whether that be cooler temperatures, direct sunlight, or wind.

Cold frame options

The cheapest option is to build your own cold frame from recycled materials, and I have provided a suggested blueprint and instructions for doing so on pages 26–29.

If you decide to buy a cold frame premade, prices will range considerably depending on construction materials. A simple structure made of soft wood and plastic will cost a good deal less than an aluminum or hardwood structure clad in glass.

Traditionally, a cold frame was a predominantly brick-built structure attached to the sunny side of a greenhouse to support the cultivation of the plants within. This style is still available to buy but may require a contractor to construct it for you, making it one of the more expensive options. If you have the ability to build a cold frame with a brick base yourself, or the budget to hire someone to do it for you, the benefit is the warmth that the bricks capture during the day and release at night, giving your plants a little extra protection during the winter and early spring, when sharp frosts can pose a problem.

Cold frame structures

Cold frames can be one- or two-sided, either with a solid back and one sloping, transparent lid or structured like a miniature house with two sloping, transparent lids that meet at the apex of the "roof," offering greater light transmission. If your cold frame is positioned against a wall or the base of a greenhouse, then a one-sided cold frame will be the more practical option. Freestanding cold frames can be accessed from all sides, making the double-sided roof more applicable.

However you construct your cold frame, ensure that it has plenty of ventilation to avoid disease and rot. When temperatures begin to rise, greater air movement is essential to help plants grow more rapidly and healthily. To achieve this, your cold

A cold frame can act as a transitional growing space between the protected greenhouse and the exposed garden.

"Cold frames offer that transitional bridge from the greenhouse to the garden by allowing you to acclimatize plants to harsher conditions."

Ventilation is key to plant health, so a cold frame with an adjustable lid is essential.

frame lid should be able to open to varying degrees, either through a simple set of wood pieces cut to different lengths to prop the lid open or by more complex mechanisms and levers.

When to move plants to a cold frame

Seedlings and plants that have been recently pricked out (see page 94) are often too fragile to be placed in a cold frame. The cooler temperatures and cold winds of early spring can be damaging for young plants. As a rule, I wait until my pricked-out plants have rooted in their cell trays or small pots before I expose them to the harsher conditions. Cold frames should be an acclimatizing tool for plants that will then be ready to plant out.

During the summer, cold frames can offer a cooler environment compared to greenhouses, making them ideal for bringing along younger plants, such as germinating seedlings, which would otherwise be compromised by the high temperatures in the greenhouse.

Hardening off

Hardening off is the process of gradually exposing young plants that have been raised in a greenhouse to colder temperatures, stronger airflow, and lower humidity for a week or two, until they are robust enough to cope with outside conditions. A cold frame is the ideal piece of equipment for this.

Construct a cold frame

A wooden-sided cold frame is easy to build and can be constructed out of reclaimed materials. This is a good way to save money while being conscious of sustainability. Though it depends on how elaborate your design, most basic structures can be built in a few hours.

For this project, I recycled some wooden pallets and an old window. Wooden pallets are often plentiful and easily obtained from local or online marketplaces. I found that the uniform size of the precut timbers was helpful when it came to building a cold frame. This can be easily replicated by buying timber from a builders' merchant, but your costs will increase.

If you choose to recycle a window to provide the lid for your cold frame, the window will then dictate the size of your structure. Polycarbonate sheets and glass can also be used to top your frame, in which case, the dimensions of your frame can be adjusted to suit your needs or space. When constructing your frame, the objective is to have the back panel higher than the front, with sloping sides to allow water to drain away and to maximize the potential for light to transmit through the top. Any timber that is used should be treated to prolong the life of the frame; this can be an annual task to maximize the lifespan of your structure. Wood-preserving oils, paints, and stains will all help extend the life of your cold frame. Your choice will be governed by the finish you desire. A series of individual cold frames will give you greater flexibility if you need more space, or creating a single cold frame with two windows that operate as individual vents is also an option.

Tips

- If recycling a window, avoid any with signs of rotten wood.
- If your cold frame will be of a size that is difficult to move, construct the frame in place, as a glass-topped frame will be heavy.
- Make sure that the slats of your pallets are of equal width to make calculations and measurements much more straightforward.

Basic construction

The reclaimed window I used for this project dictated its dimensions, but you can adjust these measurements to suit your own space and materials. The same construction principles will apply.

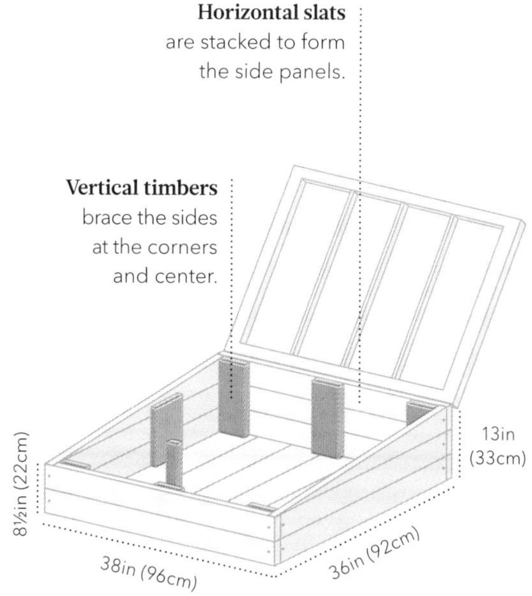

A DIY cold frame constructed from recycled materials can be tailored to fit your space.

Equipment

- Tape measure
- Reclaimed window
- Pencil
- Sandpaper (optional)
- Exterior wood paint (optional)
- 2–3 wooden pallets
- Tools to disassemble a pallet (large flat-headed screwdriver or claw hammer, crowbar, or pallet breaker)
- Wood saw
- Screwdriver (preferably electric)
- Screws (enough to secure the panels and attach the sides; the number will depend on the size and height of your cold frame)
- Large triangle
- 2 hinges

Instructions

Getting started

Measure the window and work out the dimensions of your cold frame accordingly. You should ensure that the window will sit comfortably on top of your frame, and remember that the back panel should be higher than the front. To aid the efficient run-off of rainwater, any beaver-tailed panes or overlapping glass should be positioned so the higher panes sit above the lower, allowing water to run down from top to bottom without pooling and away from the plants.

01

If the paintwork of the window is tired and in need of repair, sand down the frame, removing the loose paint, and repaint with an exterior paint product in the color of your choosing.

02

Break up the wooden pallets, using a flat-headed screwdriver or claw hammer to pry the slats from the frame. Knock through any nails and reuse them if possible. Try to save as much timber as possible for the sides, front, back, and bracing timbers of your cold frame. Cut the slats and bracing timbers to the lengths you require using a wood saw. Remember that the bracing timbers for the side panels should vary in length to accommodate the sloping sides.

03

Now build the front and back panels. To create the downward-sloping angle of the lid, the back panel should be one slat higher than the front. Arrange the horizontal slats on a level surface and attach vertical brace timbers to them (often two or three, depending on the size of the cold frame), screwing through to each slat.

04

Assemble one side panel, using the same number of horizontal slats as the lower front panel (in this case two slats), and attach to the back and front panels at the corners with screws. To match the height of the side panel to the taller back panel at one end and the lower front panel at the other, cut another horizontal slat diagonally in half. When you attach it to the top of the side panel, the wider end of the cut slat should match the taller back section and the thinner end should marry up with the lower front, creating a slope.

05

Repeat this process for the other side panel and secure all four sides together at the corners with screws, ensuring the structure is square with a triangle. Before tightening the screws, make sure that the lid sits well on the frame.

01

06

Attach the lid with two hinges, enabling you to lift it comfortably and securely.

07

Use a small piece of leftover pallet timber, here 12in (30cm) long, to create a prop to hold open the lid for ventilation. Attach it loosely to the middle of the front panel so it pivots on the screw. When a cooler environment is needed, use two longer pieces of timber to prop up the lid in the two front corners for increased air circulation.

02
03
04
05
06
07

Cloches

A mini-greenhouse with adjustable ventilation can act as an effective cloche to protect young plants.

Cloches help make the transition from the greenhouse or cold frame to the garden less stressful for young plants by insulating them from cooler temperatures and preventing the soil from being permanently saturated.

Traditionally, cloches were bell-shaped structures made from glass—*cloche* meaning "bell" in French—which could cover tender young plants in the ground, offering protection in the spring when temperatures can fluctuate and still get close to freezing.

The benefits of cloches

Cloches offer a few key benefits for plants in the garden:

- They raise the soil and air temperature and increase humidity within the structure, all of which will accelerate seed germination compared to growing in open ground. Position your cloche one week before you sow your seeds to allow time for the soil and air temperatures to rise.
- Such raised temperatures extend the growing season in early spring, meaning that we can sow tender salads and herbs, such as dill, cilantro, and summer lettuce, a month or so earlier than in open ground.
- Heat loss is reduced at night within the cloche. This means that early crops are protected, and the extra heat extends the growing season of late-performing crops such as chilies, peppers, and eggplants, which can become less productive when temperatures fall.
- Cloches create a physical barrier against garden pests, such as pigeons, mice, and butterflies.
- Dry foliage can be more disease resistant; cloches keep sensitive plants like tomatoes dry at night, which reduces the risk of blight caused by wet foliage. Regardless of the style and fabric of your cloche, ventilation is crucial to encourage healthy plants, as high humidity can lead to disease and rot, and so increase air flow as the plant matures. Simple cloches can be propped up at the base with a stone or brick to allow increased air movement from underneath.
- Zucchini and pumpkins can be vulnerable to frost when first planted out; cloches will provide protection for those young plants until temperatures become more ambient.
- Cold winds can reduce growth rate, so the protection of a cloche will promote soft growth, which is beneficial for early salad crops. Good air flow through the vents will help toughen up the leaves a little and reduce disease.

Choosing your cloches

Plastic cloches are reusable and lightweight but must be pinned down to prevent them from blowing away, particularly in exposed gardens. Bell-shaped cloches offer great flexibility, as they can be placed wherever the need arises to protect individual plants or groups. Tunnel cloches are commonly used to protect rows of young plants (see overleaf). These structures can be clad with plastic, fleece, or mesh, depending on the need to protect from temperature or pests. Taller cloches can also be used to create a warmer summer environment for plants such as peppers, sweet potatoes, and eggplants in the summer.

There are many options available to gardeners when it comes to cloches, as they vary in robustness and cost. Cloches constructed of glass and metal, if well maintained, look great and will last a lifetime but are the most expensive option. Plastic alternatives are more affordable and, when cared for, are reusable, but even the most careful gardener may need to replace a plastic cloche after a few years.

Around young children and pets, glass cloches may be more of a hazard and are expensive to replace. If plastic structures are damaged, it won't break the bank to buy a substitute. If you're on a tight budget, you can even make your own by recycling plastic water bottles. Simply cut off the bottom of the bottle, then push it into the soil around the plant. Remove the lid to aid air movement and release warm, humid air from within the cloche.

Cloches can range from mini-greenhouses, to covered tunnels, to repurposed plastic water bottles.

Make a cloche tunnel

If budget and flexibility are key considerations and you're looking to protect rows of valuable crops, try making your own cloche tunnel.

A homemade cloche tunnel can be adjusted and moved at will and opened for ventilation.

A mobile cloche tunnel made of transparent plastic sheeting is not only easy and affordable to make, but can also be effortlessly moved around the garden as you rotate your crops.

Bendable irrigation pipes from agricultural merchants make ideal and cost-effective hoops for the tunnel. Using these, along with plastic sheeting, also allows us the flexibility to alter the height and width of the tunnel to suit the crop. For example, a double row of lettuces will require a wider tunnel without the need for much height, but a row of peppers will need a much taller tunnel to provide sufficient height and air movement, especially during the heat of the summer.

While helping manage the extremes of cold temperatures and protect crops from wind and pests, the cloche tunnel also creates a barrier against rainfall and pollinators. So, once it is in place, be mindful of watering and in some cases feeding regularly. And when it comes to the pollination of strawberries and other crops such as zucchini, ensure that your tunnel is well ventilated to allow those beneficial insects to visit your plants. The sides can be rolled up to allow for this.

Size is another important consideration. Aim for a bed that is approximately 4ft (120cm) wide so you can access the center of the cloche easily from each side. A tunnel with a height of 2ft (60cm) will be adequate to grow most salad crops and leafy herbs, but peppers, eggplants, and larger chili plants will benefit from a tunnel of approximately 2½–3¼ft (80–100cm) in height.

Equipment

- Polyethylene water pipe (10- to 12-bar irrigation piping is ideal)
- Bamboo canes cut to 12in (30cm) in length
- Transparent plastic sheeting
- Heavy-duty galvanized wire
- Wire cutters

Instructions

01
First, plant out your rows of young plants. Then cut the required number of lengths of pipe long enough to form an arch that straddles the row(s) comfortably at a height of at least 2ft (60cm).

02
Insert the bamboo canes into each end of the pipe lengths for additional anchorage in the soil.

03
Insert the bamboo canes at the ends of each arch into the soil at equal spacings, about every 1½ft (50cm) along the bed, to form arches over the plant rows. This should allow space for your plants to grow with a reasonable amount of air movement.

04
Cut a piece of transparent plastic sheeting to the required length and width to cover the arches, allowing enough surplus to be able to roll up the material along the sides and at each end to create a good seal, preventing access by rabbits, birds, and slugs. Lay the plastic centrally over the pipe hoops.

05
Cut 8in (20cm) lengths of heavy-duty galvanized wire and bend them into U-shaped pins. Push the pins into the ground to attach the rolled plastic edges to the soil around the perimeter of the tunnel.

06
On warm days, gather the plastic on the opposite side from the prevailing wind, roll it up, and attach it with a few clothes pegs to open one side of the tunnel. This will allow for air movement and help prevent disease and rot, and also provide access so you can tend to your plants.

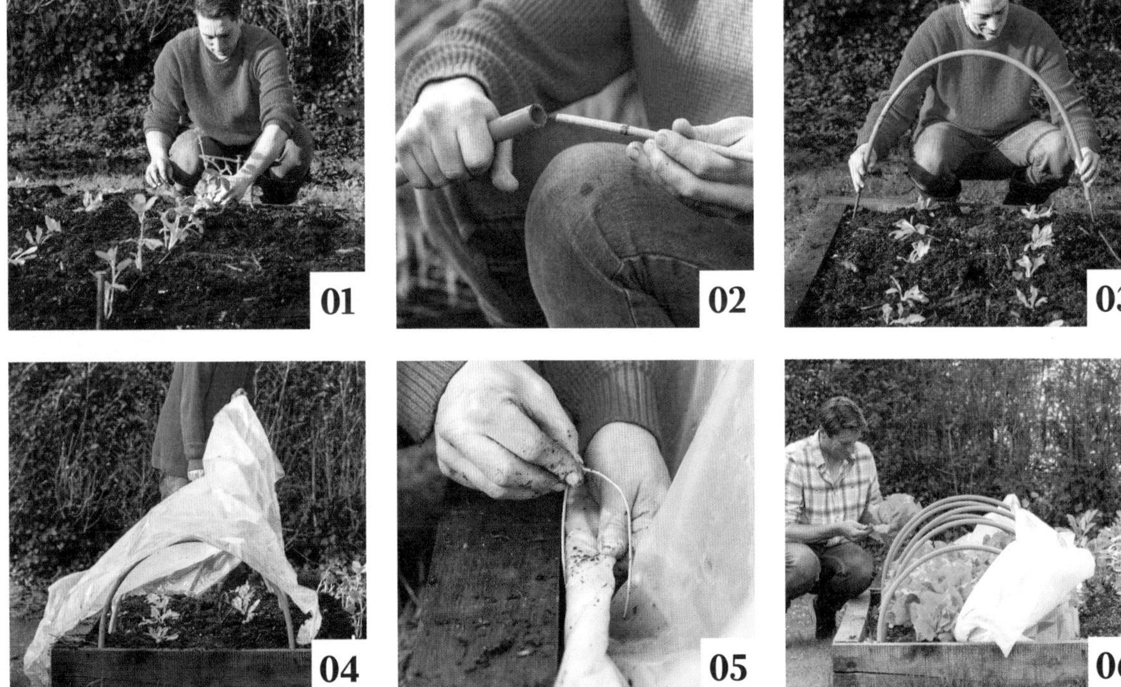

Practicalities such as site planning, design, budget, and construction choices all come together to make a successful greenhouse complex.

Planning and design considerations

The first considerations when planning a greenhouse are where to put it for optimum plant growth and convenience and how to integrate the structure into your garden. Get these fundamentals right, and your journey toward greenhouse growing will be off to flying start.

Where you situate your greenhouse will have implications for how well your plants grow, how your garden looks, and how you use it. You should consider the practicalities of how accessible your greenhouse is on a daily basis, the best position in terms of light and shelter, as well as any approvals and permits you might need from your local authority. It's also important to think about the impact on your neighbors, both residential and on allotment sites.

Rules and regulations

Erecting a greenhouse is a commitment of your time and a lot of work, so it is always worth checking any local planning or zoning regulations before you commit to a purchase. On the whole, greenhouses don't require planning permission, as they are usually classed as permitted developments. Putting one in your front garden, or building a particularly large structure that takes up a lot of outdoor space, may require permission from your local authority, so get clarification before you begin to build.

Greenhouses that are built near public footpaths or are close to or part of a historical building are likely to require permission, so again, take a cautious approach and check with your local authority before you progress too far. It's also wise and considerate to let your neighbors know that you'll be putting up a greenhouse to avoid any unnecessary conflict once the structure is built.

Rules and regulations also apply to allotment sites, so check with your local authority or allotment committee if any written permission is needed for you to add a greenhouse to your plot before the spade goes in the ground. Good neighborly relations are just as important in an allotment community as they are in your residential one.

Where to place your greenhouse

There are numerous factors to consider when deciding where to put your greenhouse.

Light levels

To get the best from your greenhouse all year round by maximizing light levels, orient your greenhouse from east to west, if you can. One that is oriented from north to south will absorb a good level of light during the summer but may struggle to achieve good light levels in spring.

To this end, avoid placing your greenhouse in the shadow of any buildings or trees. Any shade cast over the greenhouse can inhibit growth or cause that growth to be leggy and weak, especially during winter and spring, when light levels are lower.

Maximize your greenhouse's capabilities by choosing the best possible place for it.

Shelter

It's sensible to situate your greenhouse away from prevailing winds, in a sheltered spot in the garden. During high winds and storms, you don't want to be fretting over whether your greenhouse is safe. Likewise, avoid positioning it under any trees, as they naturally shed branches, which will damage your greenhouse.

Cold air will travel down a slope in the same way that water will, so also avoid positioning your greenhouse at the bottom of a slope, particularly a north-facing one, as this is likely to be a frost pocket, which will have a detrimental effect on your plants during the winter and early spring.

Accessibility

Bear in mind that you need to have access to your greenhouse on a daily basis. If it is placed a long way from your house or behind an area strewn with obstacles, you may soon resent the long or difficult trudge to check on your plants, especially if you have mobility issues. To avoid this, find a spot that is easily accessible, install a hard path across any lawn you have to cross, and clear any access routes of debris or overgrown plants to make going back and forth easier.

Access to services

If you intend to have electricity in your greenhouse or an irrigation system that runs off utility water, this may have a bearing on its destination, too. Providing power and water to a greenhouse can be expensive and lots of work, so aim to reduce labor and costs by positioning it close to services. Fear not, though: If you do not have the budget to connect the structure to water or electricity, most people—including those who rent properties—make do perfectly well with watering cans and isolated heaters.

Clear a path to your greenhouse, or put a small lean-to near your back door, for easy access.

Where to put a greenhouse

Practical matters such as light, shelter, and accessibility should all be considered when deciding where to place your greenhouse.

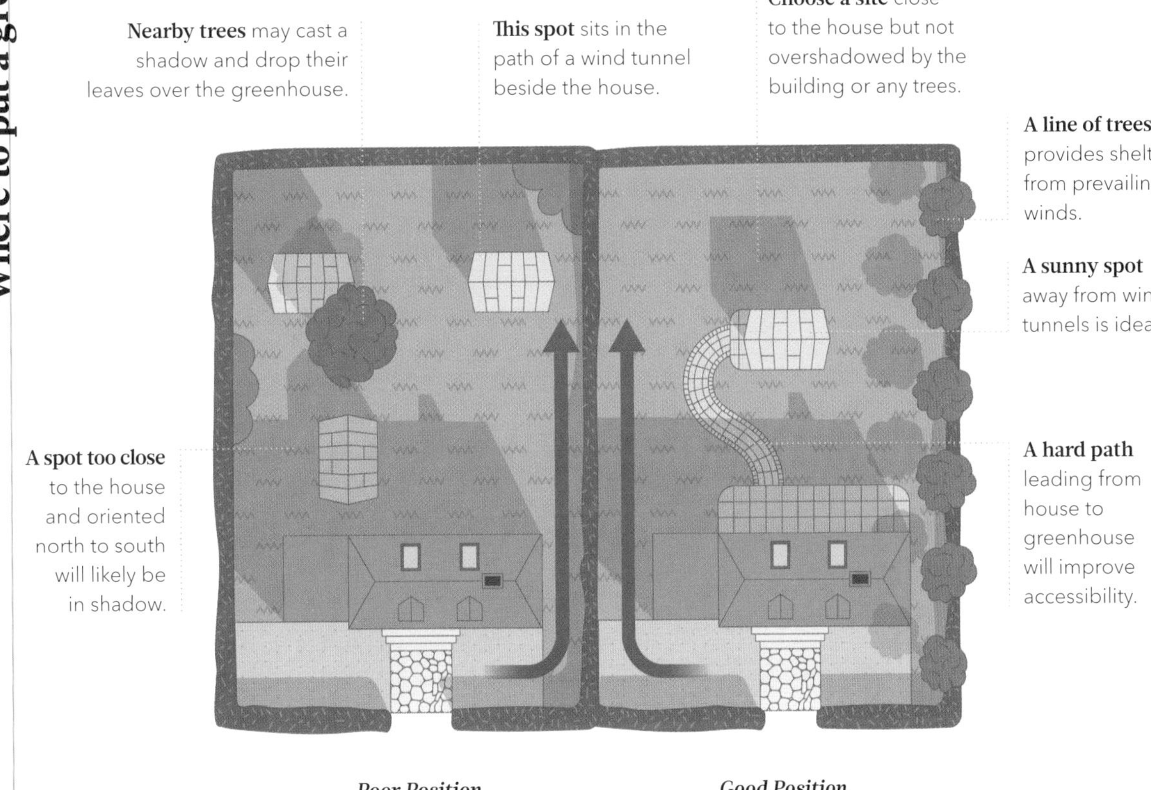

Poor Position

Good Position

Integrating a greenhouse into a garden design

Greenhouses don't have to be purely functional spaces; they can be designed to work in tandem with your garden, and even enhance its design. You can choose the materials you use for the structure, for example, based on aesthetic preference or how they unite with your house and the rest of your garden. Think, also, about the size and proportion of your greenhouse in relation to the rest of your garden and how much of a feature you want it to be in the overall design.

Greenhouses can also be easily absorbed into the garden scheme by softening their hard lines with planting in beds, borders, and containers around the structure (though make sure, of course, that these plants do not cast a shadow over the greenhouse). Raised beds full of cut flowers or vegetables can look very in keeping with your greenhouse and the functionality of the space, not only adding texture and color, but contributing to the overarching theme in that part of the garden. Such considered planting gives your working area an opulence and softness, especially during the summer months.

Paving slabs are a good foundation for large greenhouses, while soil works well for smaller structures.

Construction techniques

Before you get carried away by all the planting possibilities in your new greenhouse, one of the most important first steps is to focus on the foundations and the way in which you will build your structure.

Once you have selected the site for your greenhouse, it's time to decide what kind of foundations it will sit upon and how you (or someone else) will build it. If you have purchased a greenhouse second-hand, now is the time to assess how to dismantle and reconstruct it, as well as fit and replace any panes of glass.

Foundations

It is hugely important that the foundations for your greenhouse are square and level, particularly with larger greenhouses, as the way the structure is fitted together and aligns can be very sensitive. An uneven base will cause you nothing but headaches when it comes to the build. It's best to assess your building abilities and be honest with yourself when deciding whether to engage a contractor–who will have machinery and lasers to ensure the levels are spot on–for this part of the construction, or whether to attempt it yourself.

Options for foundations

What you plan to grow, the size of your greenhouse, and accessibility to the area will all play a part in your choice of foundation material. As long as the structure sits level, you can adopt one or a combination of the options that follow to achieve your desired finish.

- **Concrete pad** A durable, long-lasting option, but expensive compared to other options. Depending on the size of your greenhouse, concrete can be mixed in a wheelbarrow; cement mixer; or, for larger areas, a cement truck (access will need to be considered for the latter). Bear in mind that you will only be able to grow plants in containers or raised beds.
- **Soil** The easiest and cheapest foundation to implement, with just four concrete posts in the ground at each corner to secure the frame. You can use the existing soil to create growing beds, as well as compacted areas for pathways. This option is not suitable for larger greenhouses.
- **Paving slabs** A decorative, long-lasting option. Using either recycled or new slabs in natural or reconstituted stone, a variety of finishes can be achieved. Provides a solid base, but one that allows water to drain away between the slabs.
- **Perimeter base** You can create a solid base with slabs, breeze blocks, bricks, or railway sleepers to attach the greenhouse frame to, using fewer materials than a solid floor. Can be easily moved and allows for growing beds within the greenhouse.

Self-build or go professional?

If you have chosen a custom design for your greenhouse, professional contractors will construct this unique structure for you. Most greenhouses, however, are bought as prefabricated kits, and here you have the option to either engage a contractor

to assemble it for you or to build it yourself. The cost of hiring professional contractors may initially be off-putting, but this is another opportunity to put your skills under the microscope. Do you have the logic and patience required to construct a greenhouse, particularly a second-hand one that may be missing parts?

In a standard greenhouse kit, you are provided with all the equipment you need. And although it may arrive in what seems to be hundreds of boxes, by methodically reading through the instructions and allowing yourself plenty of time, constructing the kit yourself is very achievable with the support of a friend or partner. Most will suggest that the sides are constructed first, followed by the roof, and finally the glazing. If you're not confident about doing this, however, your supplier will be able to recommend a contractor who can build your greenhouse for you. These contractors are experienced and, although there'll be a cost implication, the standard of finish should be high and the process will be much quicker.

The other alternative is building or customizing your own greenhouse from scratch, from raw materials instead of a kit. This can be an incredibly rewarding experience, but before you embark on such a project, ask yourself: Do you have the time, expertise, and money to pull all the different components together to create a stable structure where you can grow plants successfully? Remember that details such as ventilation, heating, staging, and light transmission all need to be considered.

Second-hand construction

If you have bought your greenhouse second-hand, you may need to dismantle it in order to transport it from its original home, then reconstruct it in your own garden. This may sound daunting, especially as the manufacturer's instructions are likely to have long since disappeared, but if you are prepared and methodical in your approach, it can be done successfully. See overleaf for some guidance that will help you if you decide to attempt it yourself. Alternatively, local greenhouse suppliers should be able to provide details of recommended contractors who can erect second-hand greenhouses.

How to dismantle and rebuild a second-hand greenhouse

Dismantle the greenhouse in the biggest pieces possible, take lots of photographs and notes, and make sketches while you take it apart. It's also important to number the panes of glass as you go. Wear heavy-duty gloves, and remove any obstacles or trip hazards from the area while maneuvering the glass. Old towels, blankets, and bedding are always handy when transporting panes of glass, and a few helpers are also very useful. The process should be methodical, following the order below:

- Work from the top down, removing the glass panes from the roof and then the sides, saving any clips. When removing the side glass, tip the top of the pane toward you until level with the ground, then pass to a helper to pack safely.
- Detach vents and doors, sliding doors off the tracks. Vents should lift and slide out of the frame. Automatic openers should be removed before the vents.
- Dismantle the roof frame in the biggest sections possible. Remember, the less you dismantle, the less you'll have to rebuild.
- Dismantle the sides of the frame, retaining as many nuts and bolts as possible. When one side is detached from the main frame, lower it slowly to the ground.
- When rebuilding, reverse the steps, making sure that you've purchased extra clips and fixings to cover all eventualities.

With the right tools and a few basic skills, you can dismantle, construct, and repair a small greenhouse yourself.

How to fit glass panes

This process of fitting glass panels will apply to assembling a new greenhouse and also reconstructing a second-hand one. It's a useful skill to have for ongoing maintenance of your greenhouse, too. Even the most careful person can break a pane or two, and swift, safe repairs are essential, particularly before the stormy weather associated with fall arrives.

01
Offer up the glass pane to the frame, tipping the top slightly toward you. I find that suction pads are incredibly useful during this process.

02
Depending upon your greenhouse kit, sit the pane into the clips or joins that marry the glass panels together or the panel to the frame.

03
Slot the glass pane into the frame and position vertically, always maintaining contact with the glass.

04
Use a pair of pliers or your fingers to attach a clip to the sides of the pane, securing the glass to the frame. Don't scrimp on the clips; the more secure the glass, the better.

01

02

03

04

Doors and ventilation

Standard greenhouse kits will include sliding doors with tracks above and below for the door(s) to run along easily.

Accessibility and air movement are hugely important considerations when constructing your greenhouse. You will be using the doors and vents daily; get it wrong, and you'll be kicking yourself while you struggle to squeeze a wheelbarrow through a narrow doorway or find yourself battling to stave off plant pests and diseases that thrive in a stuffy, airless environment.

A well-functioning greenhouse requires both spatial accessibility for your own convenience and effective ventilation for the health of your plants. Easy access to your greenhouse is essential for any gardener, but particularly for wheelchair users and those with mobility issues. If you have the scope (in terms of both space and budget) for double doors, then I'd recommend it, from a practical standpoint. Smaller greenhouses with single doors are perfectly adequate for many, but they can be difficult to negotiate with a wheelbarrow or wheelchair and are better suited to transporting only modest quantities of materials in and out at a time.

Once the practicalities of access are resolved, pay particular attention to the way in which air will move around the inside of your greenhouse. Although a few plants—such as tropical orchids and palms, cucumbers, melons, and eggplants—will enjoy a warm, humid environment to grow in, the majority of plants rely on drier, gentle air movement to promote healthy growth and avoid fungal diseases, rot, and pests. Ventilation is one of the best tools for growing plants successfully, and whether it be via roof vents, side vents, or louvres, consider this vital element carefully. It is better to have more ventilation than you first imagine you might need, as they can be brought in and out of commission when needed, compared to not having the option at all. If you are building your own greenhouse, factor in ventilation as one of the fundamental aspects of your design.

Doors

If you're buying a greenhouse from new, it may be sold as a standard kit, with the ability to add additional ventilation and modifications to your doors, such as double doors, at an extra cost. The size of your greenhouse is a factor, as most large structures will give you the option of double doors.

Hanging a door

Whether it be a prefabricated kit or a disassembled, second-hand greenhouse, it is best to build your door and add the glass before you attempt to hang it. Trying to glaze a hung door is difficult and dangerous, so it is advisable to work safely from a table or the ground using screws, nuts, and bolts, which should either be provided with the kit or sourced before assembling your DIY greenhouse door. There will often be a track at the top of the frame from which the door hangs and slides (in the case of a kit), often with a wheel that travels along that track. The bottom of the door frame also runs along a track, with a lip creating a tension that holds the door in place. The door(s) slide from left to right and are stopped at the end of the track by rubber caps to prevent the door from coming off. Keep your door mechanisms and tracks clear and always lubricated for easy movement.

A partition wall can be added to larger greenhouses, allowing for different temperate zones.

Partition walls

Larger greenhouses may have the option of adding a partition wall, with an extra set of doors for access. These partitions are perfect for zoning your greenhouse, to create different environments within the same structure. Tomatoes and cucumbers are two of the most popular plants that we choose to grow in our greenhouses, but both require quite different growing conditions. Cucumbers grow better in a warmer, humid environment, whereas tomatoes require a much brighter, well-ventilated space. A partition wall will allow you to create two very different environments and grow those two crops successfully at the same time.

When it comes to managing your greenhouse in the winter, a partition can also reduce the volume of air you need to heat, making your heaters far more efficient. In my larger greenhouse I have used the smaller partitioned-off section at the back as my overwintering and propagation area. This has allowed me to protect young, vulnerable seedlings and tender plants against the extreme cold temperatures with a heater, which requires less energy or fuel to heat that small space than it would the whole greenhouse.

Partition walls with doors included can be purchased as part of a prefabricated greenhouse kit. Alternatively, a cheaper option would be to hang a strong transparent plastic sheet from floor to ceiling, with a slit down the center for access, creating a partition curtain.

Ventilation

When the vents and doors are open, fresh air is drawn through your greenhouse. As the hot air inside rises and the cooler air from outside falls, the airflow circulates around the plants, eventually exiting the greenhouse, taking heat and a little moisture with it. This refreshing airflow is important for healthy growth, as well as reducing pests and diseases. Most greenhouses will have adequate ventilation to support plant growth, but electric fans can be added to increase air circulation if mold and disease become an issue when growing.

Roof vents

Look at your ventilation options and ensure that you have several vents in your roof space. I would suggest roof vents that represent around 20 percent of the overall floor space. Heat will escape your greenhouse through the roof space and, in the height of summer especially, having that increased ability to disperse warm air is critical.

When it comes to the mechanics of roof ventilation we have a couple options. The first is manual ventilation where you raise and lower the vents by hand, depending on the conditions. You have far more control over these manual vents than you do over automatic types. Automatic ventilation uses a salt solution or wax that expands as it heats up. The expansion of the liquid engages a piston that opens the vent, and when the temperature cools the liquid contracts and closes the vent. These types of vents are useful for people who are not at home during the day and therefore cannot react to changes in temperatures as needed.

The other consideration is the height of your greenhouse. Some greenhouses are much taller than the gardeners who grow within them. In these cases, automatic ventilation may be preferable, as it takes away the need to use a stepladder to reach the top vents.

Roof vents in your greenhouse are essential. A mechanism for opening them manually (or automatically) can be fixed in place once constructed.

Installing a roof vent

Different models of greenhouse may vary but you need to assemble the roof vents and install them before you glaze the roof. The majority of ventilation panels are installed by sliding them along a track and, once in position, they are secured and can be levered open. Automatic and manual vent openers can be connected at the end of the build.

Side ventilation and louvre vents

Side vents and louvre vents allow gentle airflow in and around your plants. You want to avoid cold drafts, which can often be created by opening doors and vents too much, early in the season. I tend to think of venting my greenhouse in three different stages:

1. If the temperatures begin to rise then I add a little side ventilation, creating gentle air movement.
2. The second level of ventilation is to open the roof vents, which allows the excessive warm air to escape and increases that airflow even further.
3. On very warm days the third level of ventilation comes through opening the doors. Opening them just a little creates a small draft and increases air circulation, and by opening them fully you allow more air movement. On warm days, however, the draft that comes through the doors isn't cold and damaging because the ambient temperature outside is high. Often the late morning on a warm, still summer day is the right time to open your doors, closing them toward the early evening to trap that warmth in your greenhouse before the temperatures fall a little.

Installing a louvre vent

Louvre vent frames are added when the side glass is attached; in the case of prefabricated kits, they often replace a pane of glass and should be assembled in advance. Strips of glass are added or slotted into the louvre frame after the sides are glazed, as one of your last jobs in the glazing process. Louvre vents are positioned near to the floor to encourage cool air to enter the greenhouse and rise as it warms. If you are constructing your own greenhouse, louvre ventilation panels can be purchased online and added to your frame, alongside your glass panels and windows.

Glass strips should be added to louvre vent frames at the end of construction. These vents can be operated manually.

Determining optimum ventilation

The avoidance of cold drafts is crucial during the winter and spring, and the knack of increasing and decreasing air movement is an art that comes with experience. Generally, as temperatures increase, so too can the amount of air movement you introduce.

Of course, we also want to harness solar power for optimum plant growth. This means allowing the greenhouse to heat up gently in the morning to the point where it starts to feel a little uncomfortable. This allows the greenhouse to build up to a temperature where the plants are growing well, but now we need to decrease that temperature and add some air circulation.

The level of ventilation you introduce will depend on the day and the wind direction. Use your instincts to gauge whether you still need to raise the air temperature by reducing ventilation or whether it's time to bring the temperature down by increasing the airflow and adding some water to the floor to cool the atmosphere (see page 114).

Toward the end of the day, when all of that solar energy is held within the greenhouse and the ambient temperature is warm, we start to close the vents and the doors to retain the heat and allow our plants to actively grow further on into the early evening, ready to start the process all over again the next day. So not only are we extending the season by growing plants under glass, we are also extending the active growing part of the day.

Mastering ventilation, knowing when to open vents to increase air movement and when to build warmth from the sun, is key to plant health.

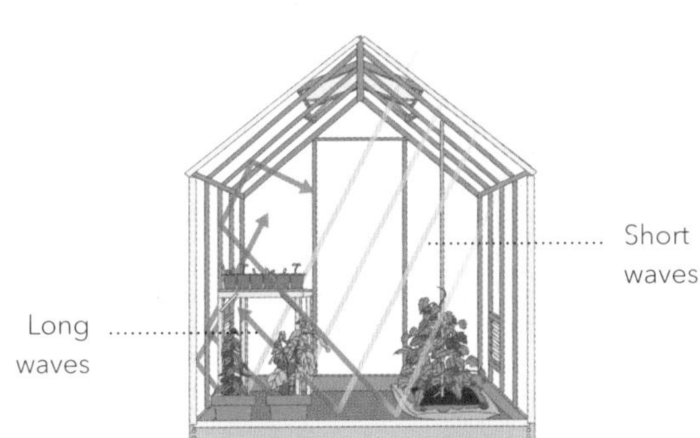

Greenhouses harness solar energy, which passes through the glass as short-wave radiation. Heat is then reflected around the inside of the structure as long-wave radiation, and when this radiation cannot escape, heat builds up inside the structure.

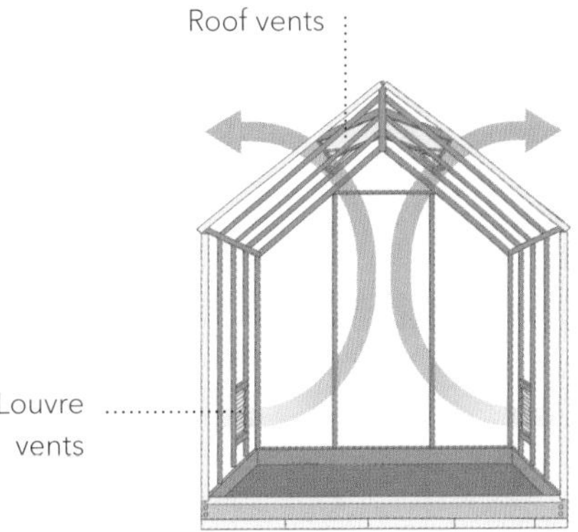

When vents are open cool air is gently drawn through the lower louvre vents at the sides of the greenhouse as the warm air rises and escapes through the roof vents. This is known as passive ventilation.

Floors and pathways

The way in which you move around the space within your greenhouse is worth taking some time over. The flooring you choose is a fundamental decision that will affect the practical way you use the greenhouse each day.

There are some practical factors that impact the type of flooring you choose for your greenhouse—primarily, cost and the enduring nature of the material are worth considering. If you are in rented accommodations and cannot install a concrete floor, then weed membrane and gravel would be more appropriate, while soil floors are essentially free, barring the cost of any soil improver. Another key decision is whether to pave the entire floor surface or leave it mainly as open soil. If you decide to cover the whole floor with slabs, bricks, or concrete, bear in mind that you will be restricted to container growing, or you will need to install raised beds. The following list will help you decide which style of flooring will best suit your growing space, your circumstances, and your budget.

Flooring tiles give a uniformity that is attractive and easy to sweep and keep clear of weeds.

Paving slabs can be drenched to boost humidity while allowing the water drain away via the gaps.

Brickwork pathways are both aesthetically pleasing and very hard-wearing.

Different types of flooring

• Soil

Securing your greenhouse directly in the soil is one of the most straightforward options, but the type of soil that you have will make a difference. For example, if you have heavy soil, every time you water your greenhouse, it will turn into a muddy mess, so the addition of a path with gravel, paving slabs, or concrete for access is advisable (see page 52).

• Weed membrane and gravel

Weed membranes or weed barriers are made of woven fabric that excludes light and physically prevents weeds from growing from the floor. Weed barriers can be swept clean and also promote drainage, making them one of the most practical and cost-effective options. The only downside is that weed membranes may need replacing after a few years, especially in heavy traffic areas, as the frayed material can sometimes create a trip hazard. Gravel can be added as a layer on top of the membrane to help preserve it and give it a more attractive finish.

• Bricks

Bricks can be one of the more expensive ways to create a floor in a greenhouse, but can also be one of the most beautiful, with recycled bricks giving a more aged finish. Brick flooring is very long-lasting and can absorb water and increase humidity.

• Concrete

A concrete floor can be expensive, particularly as you will likely need a contractor to help install it. Concrete can be a very long-term option and is also easy to maintain, but drainage needs to be considered, as water will run off the surface.

• Paving slabs

Natural stone, concrete slabs, or second-hand paving of any description can make a good greenhouse floor, with the gaps between the slabs acting as extra drainage. Paving slabs are durable and easy to maintain, and a number of second-hand slabs can be picked up cheaply from online marketplaces.

Recycled paving slabs made of either natural or reconstituted stone are easy to get a hold of and inexpensive to buy.

Laying a path

A greenhouse need not be thought of as a purely functional structure and space. Aesthetic taste and creativity can play a big part in what makes a greenhouse unique. The choice of an access path is one of those moments where you can express yourself and select whichever material or finish you love.

A pathway enables us to move safely around the greenhouse without causing compaction to the soil. The path will logically follow the most trodden or frequented route, often down the center, with space for growing on either side and toward the back.

Practical considerations

The width of the path should be determined by the distance you can comfortably reach to the back of the bed. You are aiming to conduct all of your gardening from the path without the need to tread on the soil as far as is practicable. Also consider how easy the surface will be to clean. Solid pathways can be easily swept to remove debris, whereas gravel paths can quickly become contaminated with soil and end up harboring lots of weeds.

Consider how permanent the path needs to be when choosing bedding material. Particularly if renting your home, you wouldn't want pathways that couldn't be removed with ease, and for that, a bed of dry-mix sand and cement is practical.

Avoid working directly on the soil, if possible, or lean on a spongy mat to distribute your weight. Alleviate compaction by forking over the area at the end.

Aesthetic choices

I opted for a rustic look by using recycled, natural stone paving for the path, as opposed to more utilitarian concrete slabs. My smaller greenhouse does not warrant a highwaylike path, and a series of roughly square, blocklike stones were suitable for my needs, with a finish that appeals to me. There are numerous other possibilities:

Options for greenhouse paths

- Gravel
- Concrete
- Natural stone paving slabs (new or recycled)
- Concrete paving slabs (new or recycled)
- Bark
- Landscape fabric
- Compacted soil

Equipment

- Gloves
- String line
- Wooden pegs or bamboo canes
- Spade
- Face mask
- Wheelbarrow
- Cement
- Sharp sand
- Trowel
- Hand fork
- Recycled natural stone paving slabs
- Rubber mallet
- Level
- Brush

Instructions

01
Mark out the path with pegs and string, then dig a trench to the depth of the paving slabs plus 2in (5cm) for a bed of mortar.

02
Mix a bedding mortar of 1 part cement to 6 parts sharp sand.

03
Line the trench with 2in (5cm) of the mortar mix. Roughly level the mortar using a hand fork or rake.

04
Check the design by lightly laying the slabs, then move them to the side. Begin to lay the slabs closest to the door, using the frame of the greenhouse as a guide for your desired level.

05
Check the slabs are level as you go, manipulating the sand mix and using a rubber mallet for minor adjustments.

06
Lay subsequent slabs, using the first ones as a guide, straddling a level across neighboring slabs to avoid an uneven surface.

07
Fill in any gaps with the mortar, using fingertips and a brush to work the sand into the crevices.

08
Backfill soil around the paving and leave for 24 hours to set before walking on the path.

Staging, shelving, and potting benches

We're aiming for our greenhouses to be pleasant spaces to spend our time. When we're gardening, we need to be comfortable, so considerations around the height at which we work are very important. There are various options for staging, shelving, and benching to make the space work for you.

Benching and staging are interchangeable terms, but both describe structures that are used to grow our plants at height. Staging can refer to more permanent fixtures, whereas benching can describe temporary solutions to be used at times of growing greater numbers of seedlings and plants when more space is needed, such as in the spring and early summer. Raising the height of our plants also allows us to inspect and appreciate them with ease.

Consider whether you wish to buy staging with your structure or source it separately. The advantage of the former is that prefabricated staging can be easily assembled, fits the space, and is one less thing to think about, but the advantage of custom, homemade staging is that you can tailor the structure to suit you, your needs, and the height at which you wish to work.

Staging tends to be constructed from:
- Slatted wood or metal
- Wire or plastic-coated mesh
- Solid metal, timber, or plastic sheeting

I prefer slatted or netted staging, as this allows excess water to drain away from my plants and discourages young roots from growing outside of the tray or pot by exposing them to the air.

When it comes to the height of your staging, consider the ergonomics of spending a prolonged amount of time at your workstation. Install your staging at a height so that your back is straight and you're not stooping to tend your seedlings.

Shelving

Shelving is often narrower and positioned closer to the roof space than staging but helps maximize your growing space by making use of the vertical

Install your greenhouse staging at the most comfortable working height for you.

area. It also offers a slight benefit in terms of light and warmth, compared to those plants grown on lower tiers.

Potting benches

Potting benches or trays are fundamental pieces of greenhouse equipment to hold potting mix and to provide a solid base to work on. It's best to avoid the mess of trying to fill seed trays and plant pots on a slatted bench when much of the potting mix will end up on the floor.

There are many potting benches available online to suit all budgets and tastes. Principally, one with a lipped, solid tray at a comfortable height is desirable. A basic potting bench kit with lower shelving and storage can be bought for a very reasonable price, and there is of course potential for the more DIY inclined of us to create our own masterpiece, too. I like to work from a portable or removable potting tray, which can be placed under the staging when not in use or at times when space in the greenhouse is at a premium. Consider the height at which you choose to work and the comfortable extent of your reach. Raising a small potting tray to keep your back straight is easily done with some wooden blocks or a few terracotta pots.

Multitiered shelving is indispensable for propagation, as it makes the best use of vertical space for trays of seedlings.

In spring, when young plants are growing in abundance, shelving provides valuable extra space.

Setting up a workspace

The greenhouse isn't only about giving the right conditions to our plants. The potting area in particular is the engine room where many of our plants are tended, and it must be a lovely place to spend time and where you want to be. I often take a radio into the greenhouse with me and a lovely cup of tea to while away the hours. This means I not only connect with the benefits of nurturing young plants, but also enjoy the relaxation and sense of well-being it offers.

When you're setting up your potting area or workspace, you also want to have everything you need at your disposal for convenience—see pages 60–63 for a comprehensive guide to essential greenhouse equipment.

Seasonal workspaces

Your potting bench or workspace does not have to be stationary throughout the year. There are periods when every part of your growing area is precious—for instance, in the summer months when the greenhouse is at its most bountiful—and there's no shame in capitalizing on that. I pack away my workspace to allow room for more crops in early May and rebuild it at the end of the summer when those crops have finished.

Using a potting tray for sowing and potting can help keep your workspace tidy.

Adjustable staging can be packed away when space in the greenhouse is at a premium.

A mobile potting bench can be relocated outside in summer to maximize space and make working more comfortable for you.

The most intense period of propagation is from the fall until early summer, when space for growing young plants is crucial. With a small space, why not keep things flexible? Larger greenhouses may allow for a more permanent solution, but even then, it's worth asking yourself: Is that potting bench taking up valuable growing space?

Integrated shelving in a lean-to

Lean-to greenhouses are perfect for growing where space is limited (see page 22), and during winter and spring, their integrated shelving allows us to make use of their height to grow lots of seedlings and cuttings. Around the end of May, we can then remove or adjust the shelving to make space for taller crops, such as cordon tomatoes, cucumbers, and peppers, before reintroducing the shelving in the fall.

Integrated shelving in a lean-to greenhouse is designed to be adjusted and removed at will (above). It can be maintained all year for propagation and plants that don't require much headroom, such as some succulents, herbs, and dwarf chilies (above right); it can also be removed to make way for taller plants, such as cordon beefsteak tomatoes (right).

Maintaining the greenhouse

Once you have constructed your greenhouse space, it's important to look after it. The environment we create in our greenhouse affects our plants and can make all the difference to their health and productivity.

The likelihood is that you'll be inhabiting your greenhouse most days, opening vents and doors, and utilizing staging and pathways. Keeping your greenhouse clean, avoiding any unnecessary hazards, and maintaining any mechanisms will prolong the life of your greenhouse—avoiding major and expensive repairs through the deterioration of the framework and glass—and provide the best environment for you and your plants.

Cleanliness

Cleanliness should be at the top of your list of priorities. Poor hygiene in a greenhouse can lead to various problems, notably the proliferation of pests and diseases. Prevention is far better than cure, so the best approach is to spray plants routinely with a preventative (see page 123), maintain buoyant health through feeding (see page 82), and keep your greenhouse environment clean, inside and out.

Debris such as pollen, leaf litter, and dust will settle on your glass and be washed into your gutters when it rains. This build-up, along with rainwater that does not drain freely, will provide the right conditions for moss and weeds to grow. Physically remove any leaves or moss from your gutters to allow water to flow into your downspouts and

Washing greenhouse glass inside and out will reduce pests and increase light transmission.

storage containers. This keeps water flowing away from your structure and prevents weeds developing, which could cause damage with their roots.

During the winter, clean your glass to allow maximum light transmission, which will prevent your plants from becoming laggy and drawn. Any mossy build-up between the panes of glass can also be removed at this point, which puts your greenhouse in a good position for the new growing season in spring.

Keep mechanisms moving

Doors and vents are often used daily and will need to be maintained to keep them moving and prevent any potential damage. To keep a sliding door panel running smoothly, for example, regularly lubricate the track, or the point where two pieces of metal meet, with a wax block or lubricating spray, such as WD-40. This will protect your greenhouse frame and prevent jarring, which could lead to the glass panes being put under pressure to the point where they break. Check for and remove any debris that may settle in the tracks of your door, particularly in the winter, when soil, fallen leaves, or gravel can hinder the movement. Keep vents clean and lubricate any moving parts to prevent them from catching.

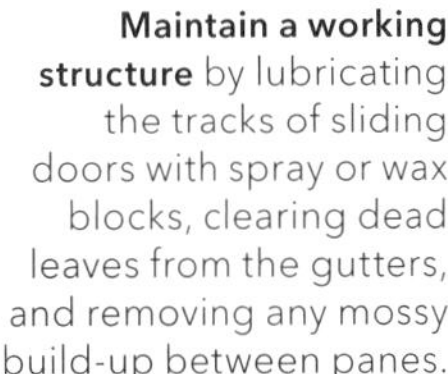

Maintain a working structure by lubricating the tracks of sliding doors with spray or wax blocks, clearing dead leaves from the gutters, and removing any mossy build-up between panes.

How to maintain a hygienic greenhouse environment

- Sweep up any spilled potting mix from the floor.
- Keep weeds to a minimum to prevent them from harboring pests.
- Wash pots and trays after each use and allow to dry before stacking neatly.
- Remove any dead or dying leaves or flowers from your plants on a regular basis, almost a few times a week, as this decay and debris will harbor fungal diseases and pests.
- Clean glass regularly to allow maximum light transition and wipe down corners to remove debris, which can harbor pests, especially after summer crops that can grow into the roof space.
- Disinfect tools such as pruners or scissors between plants with antibacterial spray to reduce the risk of transmitting viruses.
- Don’t allow areas of trash to accumulate, as these can provide ideal hiding places for slugs and snails, which will predate on your plants, causing you a great deal of frustration.
- Clean your greenhouse inside and out at least once a year.

Containers, seed trays, and basic equipment

Owning a greenhouse is all about nurturing plants and enjoying the space and processes within it, so don't waste unnecessary time running around and gathering the equipment that you need as you go. Assembling your tools and equipment beforehand will give you as much time as possible to immerse yourself in growing plants.

Essential workspace equipment

What follows is a comprehensive list of the essential items you need to start growing in your greenhouse.

Cell and seed trays

Cell trays can accommodate a variety of plants within the same tray due to each plant having its own individual cell. These trays are ideal if you only need a few of each type of plant.

Particularly deep cell trays are known as root trainers, which facilitate the development of deeper tap roots in seedlings that will grow in those trays for months instead of weeks and dislike root disturbance. These include tree seedlings; legumes, such as sweet peas and fava beans; and annual members of the carrot family, such as *Ammi majus*.

Seed trays are shallow plastic trays in which larger quantities of seed can be grown. It is possible to subdivide these large trays with split green canes to grow different plants in the same tray, but you need a very steady hand to do this. I prefer to grow each type of seed in a different pot or tray, as germination rates can vary.

Also consider seed pans, which are plastic plant pots that are wider than they are deep, though still deeper than a seed tray. This allows a large surface area for seed sowing, while the extra depth allows for stronger, longer, and more branched roots, as well as more consistent moisture levels and temperatures, leading to stronger seedlings.

Seed tray bath

Seedlings should be watered from below by using a water-holding tray, which is a gentle way to hydrate the potting mix; keeps developing seeds from being disturbed; and reduces the risk of wet seedling foliage, which can lead to damping off. Any tray that can hold water and a seed tray within it will work well. A shallow tray where the water will not come over the top of the seed tray is essential. Depending on how dry the potting mix is, most seed trays will absorb all the water they need within half an hour.

Plant pots

It's best to have a range of pot sizes—everything from 2¾in (7cm) upward—to cater to all stages of plant growth. As they grow, plants need a bigger root run from a larger pot. There is a fine balance to strike between encouraging healthy growth with a reasonable root run in a pot that doesn't dry out frequently, and avoiding overpotting into one that's too large, which can overwhelm a young plant in a sea of wet and cold potting mix.

Whether you choose terracotta or plastic pots will depend on various considerations, as both have advantages and disadvantages (see box opposite).

The greenhouse gardener's toolkit includes pots and seed trays, watering cans, plant labels, scissors, skewers, a sieve, and compost tampers.

Thermometer

A maximum and minimum thermometer is an important piece of equipment, especially in the winter and early spring, when those colder nights can catch you unaware. It is good practice to monitor and keep note of how cold your greenhouse gets at night. This will enable you to adjust your insulation and heating during the winter and to gauge how high the temperatures climb in the height of summer to inform you about shading and ventilation.

Heated propagator

A heated propagator allows you to start growing your seedlings earlier and helps with growing crops such as chilies, tomatoes, and eggplants, which require higher temperatures to trigger faster germination. Principally, the heat generated from the base of the tray accelerates the speed in which the seeds break through the compost. The added humidity that is created by the lid of the propagator helps create higher and more consistent moisture levels, which aids germination. Warmth and humidity are also beneficial when it comes to rooting cuttings successfully by encouraging root development and preventing them from drying out.

Terracotta vs. plastic pots

Your choice of pot will be determined by budget, aesthetics, mobility, and sustainability. Terracotta and plastic each have their place in gardening, with pros and cons to take into account.

Terracotta

Pros Clay pots are attractive and reusable, ideal for large displays. The porous material allows air and water to pass through, which helps gas exchange and encourages healthy root development.
Cons They are heavy, and the porosity can lead to the plant drying out faster than if grown in a plastic pot. For this reason, they aren't suited to germinating seeds.

Plastic

Pros Plastic pots can be reused many times. They are lighter and cheaper than terracotta pots and can often be sourced from others who have too many.
Cons They are less stylish than clay or metal and are not biodegradable, so avoid single-use and recycle if possible.

Peat-free potting mix

There is great debate about the effectiveness and consistency of peat-free potting mixes compared to peat-based ones, but environmentally and ethically, peat-free potting mixes are what we should all be striving to use. Most peat-free potting mixes are suitable for most plants, but the quality and constituents of the blend can vary. Aim to use a peat-free potting mix that has been developed specifically for growing plants from seed when you start sowing. Pot on young plants regularly and feed with a seaweed fertilizer to keep those young plants developing at a consistent rate. Coarser blends of potting mix are suitable for larger plants and those that are potted on beyond the cell tray stage. Universally, we should be using fresh potting mix, so avoid storing too much, and if your mix is particularly coarse, then sieve for a finer tilth.

Compost sieve

Use a sieve to remove large particles from peat-free potting mixes. Cover fine seed with sieved potting mix to improve germination rates.

Vermiculite, perlite, and sand

Perlite is created from expanded volcanic glass. When mixed with potting mix, it helps improve drainage and water absorption, adding porosity to the potting mix but no nutrition, making it ideal for rooting cuttings.

Vermiculite is a naturally occurring mineral that insulates, maintains moisture, and allows good air circulation when used to top-dress seeds.

Horticultural sand is used to add ballast and drainage to potting mixes; it is perfect for cacti and succulents. Topping plants or large seeds with sand also helps insulate, retain moisture, and prevent weed growth in perennial, shrub, and tree seeds, which may take a long time to germinate.

Labels, pencils, or pens

Although you may think that you'll remember every seed that you sow or cutting that you take, I promise you that you'll soon forget. Write down the plant name and the date that you sowed the seed or took the cutting to assess whether you've been successful as the days and weeks go by.

Watering can

Try to have a range of cans, from small ones for young plants to a couple large 10-liter (2-gallon) cans–one for liquid fertilizers and one for rainwater.

Broken pieces of terracotta for crocks

Perfect for reducing the size of the drainage hole in large terracotta pots to prevent potting mix from escaping from the base. Assemble arched pieces of terracotta above the hole to create a barrier to the potting mix but allow excess water to drain away.

Skewers for pricking out seedlings

Wooden kebab skewers or plastic pricking-out tools will help tease fragile seedlings and their roots from seed trays into small pots to grow on.

Scissors and adhesive tape

For opening seed packets and to reseal packets to keep seeds fresh and viable.

Tailor your growing media to suit your needs, using (clockwise from top left) peat-free potting mix, vermiculite, a combination of perlite and potting mix, and sand.

Cleaning equipment

A dustpan and brush, soft broom, stiff broom, and trash can are essential items for cleaning benches, glass, and floors and to keep your workspace tidy.

Compost tamper

A piece of wood, ideally the same shape and size as your favored seed-sowing vessel, with a handle like a large stamp. Press lightly onto the potting mix to produce a flat and level surface to sow your seeds and after sowing to maximize contact between seed and potting mix.

Handheld sprayer

For applying soap- and oil-based sprays for plant health and pest prevention.

Washing plant pots and seed trays regularly is good practice for plant hygiene, helping keep pests and diseases at bay.

Sustainable practices and recycling

- Wash and reuse plastic labels by cleaning them with denatured alcohol and warm, soapy water to remove grime, pencil marks, and ink marks.
- Wash terracotta and plastic pots and trays in warm, soapy water to reuse and reduce the potential for fungal disease and pests between uses.
- Reuse spent seed-starting mix in larger pots and raised beds.
- Only sow the number of seeds that you need.
- Go peat-free. Peat bogs are vital carbon stores, habitats, and flood defenses. Gardeners can help fight climate change by using peat-free potting mix.
- Use biodegradable jute string when tying in plants.
- Only heat your greenhouse enough to keep plants alive during the winter. Soft, unseasonable growth will only encourage pests and be vulnerable to the cold if exposed.
- Use captured rainwater to water plants whenever possible, but use treated utility water for seedlings to avoid bacteria that can damage young plants.
- Using biodegradable pots to transplant young plants to the garden or larger containers saves time and plastic, but be aware that the pot must be wet when planted to break down effectively.

To clean and reuse plastic plant labels, brush with denatured alcohol to remove any ink, then wash in soapy water and wipe clean with a cloth.

Heating a greenhouse

In the colder, darker months, plants grow at a much slower rate and can take a long time to recover from temperature damage. If cold spells are forecast, you may need to heat part or all of the greenhouse to keep it frost-free. Even then, extreme cold or power cuts can test the best heaters, and it is vital to keep the root balls of plants on the drier side, not saturated.

Sustainable choices

Heating with electricity from a renewable source is the most sustainable way to keep plants cozy. We should also take steps to minimize consumption:

- Mend or replace broken panes and seal cracks.
- Screen off areas to reduce the volume of space to be heated.
- Insulate inside the greenhouse with bubble wrap.
- Apply a layer of fleece over plants during cold spells.
- Fit doors and vents well with few gaps.

Electric

The most effective means of keeping a greenhouse warm is electric heating controlled via a thermostat, but this is also the most expensive to install and may not be practical for every greenhouse. Electrical outlets should be put in around waist height to avoid unnecessary conflict with your regular watering duties. There are a number fan-based heaters available with varying degrees of power; consult the manufacturer to ascertain what power output will be needed to keep your size of greenhouse frost-free.

Kerosene

Kerosene heaters are a more mobile and less permanent solution than electric, for those who do not wish to run cables into their houses or garages. You will need to keep an eye on the weather and, when a frost is forecast, light your kerosene heaters before bed and remember to blow out the flame the following morning or when conditions warm up.

01
Fill the reservoir with fuel a few hours before you aim to light the heater, so the wicks have time to absorb the liquid. Expose enough wick to form a small flame and light the wick with long safety matches.

02
Reduce the flame by adjusting the length of the wick to stop any smoke from entering the greenhouse; a small flame is enough to give frost protection in average conditions.

03
Position the flue over the flames, using gloves to protect yourself from the hot parts of the heater.

Terracotta and candle radiator

The heat of a pillar candle is a sustainable option for keeping a lean-to or small greenhouse frost-free on very cold nights. You need a candle that will burn for a minimum of eight hours, whose gentle heat is radiated out through terracotta pots and maintained by airflow drawn up through an open brick base. It's not an exact science, and you may need to experiment with the number of heaters—larger houses may require two or three to keep plants frost-free.

01
Arrange three or four bricks in a formation that a pillar candle can sit within. Place the candle in the center of the bricks and light it with safety matches.

02
Place a first, slightly smaller terracotta pot over the candle, resting it on the bricks to allow airflow to sustain the flame.

03
Place a piece of terracotta or a terracotta plate on top of the first pot to cover the drainage hole.

04
Put a slightly larger pot on top of the smaller pot, resting it on the bricks to maintain airflow.

05
The smaller pot will warm and transfer heat to the outer pot. Blow out your candle in the morning or when temperatures reach above freezing.

01 02 03 04

05

Insulation and shading

We're trying to create conditions within the greenhouse that encourage healthy, productive growth. This means avoiding excessively cold temperatures in winter and scorching temperatures in summer.

Different plants require different temperatures within a greenhouse to grow successfully. During winter, frosts can destroy tender or overwintering plants, while in summer, the greenhouse can get so warm that it's uncomfortable to garden in and plants can be scorched or suffer drought. Through insulation and shading, however, we can reduce the impact of these intense conditions.

Insulation

Lining the interior of your greenhouse with a layer of bubble wrap before the risk of frosts (usually in October or November) will help exclude any cold drafts and retain the heat. Sheets can be secured to the inside frame using fixing clips (widely available online), and this alone will increase the temperature by a few degrees. The extra insulation, as well as keeping your plants on the dry side during the winter, will give you the best chance of taking your plants into next spring.

If your greenhouse is zoned (see page 46), you might want to insulate only part of the space. Or you can reduce its height for maximum efficiency. Heat will escape a greenhouse through the roof as warm air rises, so attaching a sheet of bubble wrap across the apex of the roof will not only trap the warm air, but also reduce the volume of air that needs to be heated within your structure, making any supplementary heating more effective.

Line your greenhouse with bubble wrap to insulate your space and monitor temperatures to ensure they don't drop below freezing in winter.

The bubble wrap will restrict the amount of light coming in to a small extent. When temperatures rise in late spring—when plants no longer require extra protection from the cold but would benefit from the extra light—remove the bubble wrap to prevent it from hindering those new shoots. Once dried, and after any debris has been removed, it can be kept and stored for reuse the following fall.

Shading

During the summer, greenhouse shading can help prevent hot, dry conditions inside that will lead to poor plant growth and pest build-up.

- **Shade paint** is applied to the outside of a greenhouse to deflect some of the sun's heat and light, helping bring the temperature down inside. Some paints may require reapplication to keep them effective through the summer. You may find thick layers provide too much of a light barrier, so some adjustments throughout the year may be necessary to account for changing light levels. The paint can then be washed off at the end of summer.
- **Shading fabric** can be adapted to different greenhouse styles and sizes. Best installed on the outside of your greenhouse, it will do the same job as the shade paint, but it is less laborious to put up and bring down and can be reused.
- **Blinds** are the most aesthetic option, but as they are internal and do not block the sun's rays from passing through the glass, they do not cool the air as much as external shading fabric does.

The way your greenhouse interacts with the light in your garden will be specific to its position on your site. Apply shading to the roof space and side that is most impacted by the sun in the first instance. As the summer heat intensifies, you may need to provide shading across the entire structure to keep internal temperatures ambient. Alternatively, you might need to decrease shading by removing fabric or washing shade paint off. Summers can vary in their intensity, so we should be in a position to dial up or down the amount of protection we give our plants to keep them healthy.

Shading fabric can be bought to fit your specific model of greenhouse, or it can be universal and cut to fit.

Shading alone will not protect your plants from intense heat. Good watering techniques (see page 112) and ventilation (see page 47) are also essential.

Essential techniques

Key considerations for growing under glass

When gardening under glass, there are certain conditions–such as light, temperature, and ventilation–that must be manipulated to achieve growing success.

We are creating an artificial environment in our greenhouses in order to get the best from our plants. As a result, how they respond will be directly linked to the conditions we provide and any variations we make to them.

Light

It is essential to maximize light transmission through the cladding of our greenhouse, whether that be glass or polycarbonate. If the panels are dirty, that will reduce the amount of light that can penetrate through to your plants, causing weak and leggy growth. In contrast, during summer, light levels can be too intense and lead to scorching, so we must restrict the amount that comes into our greenhouse to alleviate plant stress. Shading at this time of year, with netting or paint (see page 66), will create more comfortable conditions.

Water

We can't grow greenhouse plants without providing water, as they have no access to rainfall. Reacting appropriately to your plants' changing hydration needs throughout the year is a skill you will hone over time. Excessive watering during the more dormant season can lead to root rot and disease, for example, while not enough water during the highly active summer will lead to drought, causing plants to wither (see page 112).

Our greenhouses demand a great deal of this precious resource when there is often little rainfall, so we must mitigate this by harvesting as much rainwater during the winter as possible. See page 110 for more on how to achieve this using rain barrels and tanks.

Watering requires a nuanced approach, as different plants will have varying needs throughout the year.

Ensure your greenhouse has plenty of ventilation options (left), as well as a heat source during the winter (above).

Temperature

The reality for most gardeners is that their greenhouses will be bright but cool during the winter and incredibly warm in summer. We can manage these environments by choosing to cultivate the right plants for the time of year. Those bright, cool conditions are perfect for overwintering plants and growing hardier salads and herbs, as well as spring-flowering bulbs and cut flowers. In summer, we can turn our attention to more tropical plants and heat-loving crops, such as tomatoes, cucumbers, and peppers.

Ventilation

Gentle, consistent air movement around our plants will encourage healthy growth, reduce pests and diseases, and help with pollination. We must learn to manipulate ventilation according to the conditions inside and outside the greenhouse, as cold drafts in winter can be harmful to sensitive plants, but a lack of ventilation in the summer can be equally damaging, exacerbating the hot, dry conditions. See page 44 for more on how to adjust ventilation for the best results.

Overcrowding

One of the pitfalls of greenhouse growing is that we tend to overcrowd our collection of plants through sheer enthusiasm. Most plants need a reasonable amount of light to grow, so the inevitable result of overcrowding will be poor growth, but many plants also require very different conditions. Some may need higher light levels or temperatures than others, and some a drier or moister atmosphere.

We want to grow everything, but we must be realistic: We simply can't have pelargoniums, ferns, orchids, begonias, cucumbers, tomatoes, and melons in one small greenhouse and expect them all to thrive. Tomatoes, for example, prefer a warm, bright, drier atmosphere, whereas cucumbers prefer a humid environment with protection from strong light. One solution is to create a community of plants that require similar conditions. Alternatively, a partition within your greenhouse will help create tailored growing zones (see page 46).

Permanent vs. mobile planting

A mix of mobile containers and raised beds allows you to grow a wide range of plants.

When planning your greenhouse, a key question is whether you wish to grow permanent plants directly in the ground or temporary plants in mobile containers.

We all have favorite plants we like to grow every year, but having the flexibility to change what we have in our greenhouse is incredibly valuable. Switching up plantings is lots of fun and means you can grow a variety of different plants each year. Although permanent planting in greenhouse beds may seem like the easier option in terms of workload, the static nature of this planting and the potential for pest build-up can be a frustration. You may decide to grow entirely permanent or mobile plants, or, if space and budget allow, a mixture of the two.

Mobile planting

Temporary mobile plantings, particularly of annual crops and flowers, allow you to change your roster of plants throughout the year. During late winter and early spring, the greenhouse can be a hive of activity, with every conceivable space on benching, shelves, and the floor occupied by seedlings and young plants. Raised beds can be full of cut flowers and salads that thrive in the lower light levels and temperatures before making way for tomatoes and cucumbers in summer.

Some plants you may try and not wish to grow again; we all make mistakes, particularly in the intense greenhouse environment. With mobile planting, you have the opportunity to build on your successes and avoid repeating failures in the future.

Growing plants in containers does restrict their vigor to an extent, but their mobility benefits their health in other ways. With chemical controls for pests and diseases no longer ethically accepted, the ability to move plants out of the greenhouse when they become pest-ridden is very useful. Plus, changing the potting mix regularly means that any soil-borne pests are likewise removed. Growing annuals, such as tomatoes, chilies, and eggplants, and then composting them also removes pests that have built up on the stems and leaves, maintaining a cleaner environment for the next crop.

Permanent planting

Permanent plantings can require a great deal of investment in terms of training and tending, but we often reap the benefits in their abundance of fruit or flowers. After all, growing a much larger plant in a permanent spot, possibly in a greenhouse border, does increase the yield. Figs, vines, and stone fruit can all be trained within a greenhouse environment, and establishing a beautiful plant over time can be a real joy.

The majority of gardeners with fairly modest greenhouses, however, should think twice about introducing more permanent planting, as these trees and vines require lots of space. With permanent planting, gardeners also need to be more vigilant for overwintering pests, as there is a danger that the accumulation year on year of pest build-up can lead to a very lackluster plant, which may ultimately compromise the fruit you have invested so much time in.

Mobile or permanent?

	Mobile Planting	Permanent planting
Advantages	Greater flexibility	Can grow larger plants that you can invest in
	Can grow a wider range of plants	Plants will give a higher yield of fruit or flowers
	Pests can be easily removed from the greenhouse	
	Mistakes can be more rectified or replaced	
Disadvantages	Plant vigor can be compromised	More space is needed
	Plants require more tending	Pests have to be controlled culturally

Growing directly into soil

Depending upon the type of flooring you choose for your greenhouse, the layout, and the quality of the soil that you have, one option for growing plants in your greenhouse is directly into beds.

When deciding whether or not to grow your greenhouse plants directly into the soil or not, there are advantages and disadvantages to consider. Plants will behave slightly differently when grown in soil, compared to containers, due to the conditions, and the care they need from you will also differ. Depending on your soil, this may be a case of trial and error, but sound growing techniques will ensure success.

Pros and cons of growing in soil

Pros

- No need to move large volumes of potting mix by filling and emptying containers.
- More stable soil temperatures, compared to containers.
- Deeper root run for larger plants.
- Greater moisture-holding properties if mulched, compared to pots.

Cons

- Compaction and poor drainage can be an issue.
- Soils can deteriorate over time and become exhausted.
- Soil pests and diseases can build up.
- Root restriction from containers can encourage fruiting, whereas plants grown with a larger root run can be reluctant to flower.

Planting into soil gives a deeper root run and more consistent moisture levels for vigorous growth.

An organic mulch will improve soil fertility, structure, and water retention (left); working from a path avoids soil compaction (above).

Maintaining soil health

The soil within a greenhouse bed is exposed to incredibly high temperatures during summer, which can have a sterilizing effect, reducing the biological activity through heat and drought. The soil must work very hard to sustain productive plants, whether that be with fruit, flowers, or both; it is a living, breathing part of our greenhouse, and to nurture it requires a degree of husbandry and maintenance.

To maintain air movement within the soil, avoid compaction as much as possible, breaking it up with a garden or hand fork after any work on the soil. Working from wooden boards or a path to avoid contact with the soil also helps prevent compaction around your plants.

Plants use up nutrients in the soil as they grow, so between each planting or crop, we should replenish that fertility with some organic matter. This can be well-rotted compost or manure, either applied as a mulch or incorporated into the top 6in (15cm) of the soil. Given the demands on greenhouse soil, I'd recommend doing both before each new planting. Bagged potting mix will contain very little fertility; well-rotted compost or green waste from your local authority or compost supplier will provide more nutrition for your growing plants.

The soil should also be kept moist but not waterlogged to avoid anaerobic conditions, which will lead to the depletion of biological and fungal activity. Regular hydration of your greenhouse soil throughout the summer will be an important part of maintaining its health.

Mulching and weed control

Mulching our greenhouse soil has the same benefits as mulching in the garden. A 2–4in (5–10cm) layer of organic matter on the surface will suppress weed growth by eliminating light and smothering weed seeds; add fertility as it is broken down by the organisms within the soil; and reduce evaporation, locking in moisture.

Before we mulch, our greenhouse soil should be moist and weed-free. Mulching on top of dry soil has the adverse effect of locking out moisture, making it harder to saturate the rooting zone for our plants. Also, avoid using fresh, undecomposed compost or manure, as this may scorch the plants and cause nitrogen lock-up. This is when the nutrient is used to help break down the fresh material within the mulch, thereby reducing the amount of nitrogen available to the plant and starving it.

How to grow in containers

Container-grown plants offer lots of flexibility in the greenhouse. Moisture levels, nutrition, and the sharpness of the drainage can all be easily manipulated to influence how the plant grows. And being able to move plants at will can be very useful in such controlled conditions.

Containers allow us to successfully navigate the seasonal nature of growing different plants in our greenhouse. Growth can be accelerated with the introduction of food and more regular watering during late spring and early summer and withheld

Pros and cons of container growing

Pros

- You can better control the compost, fertilizer, and moisture content than when growing in soil.
- You can manipulate pot size to restrict roots to encourage flowering or limit growth.
- Mobility (for example, you can move a potted citrus into the garden for summer and back into the greenhouse in winter).
- Pots provide a warmer rooting environment in early spring.

Cons

- Pots require more frequent watering than soil.
- Fertilizer can leach out of the pot; in the ground, soil has greater retention.
- Plants experience greater extremes in temperature and moisture levels than in soil.

A combination of pots, grow bags, and hanging baskets allows for flexible, abundant growth.

Reusable grow bags (above) are hard-wearing and sustainable, while single-use grow bags (left) provide a tailored potting mix to sustain plants for one growing season. Both can support compact plants as well as climbers, such as tomatoes and peppers.

during winter to great effect in containers. From grow bags, to hanging baskets, to pots of all shapes and sizes and materials, if there is adequate drainage, almost any container can be suitable for growing plants. There are, however, distinct advantages and disadvantages compared to growing directly in the soil.

Container size

When we grow plants from seeds or cuttings, gradually moving up in pot size as they develop is essential for meeting their needs. When it comes to larger display containers or the final-sized growing container for your plant, the practicalities of size become important.

The larger the container, the more potting mix it can hold, creating a deeper root run. This larger volume of material will dry out less frequently and can support a bigger plant. Smaller containers may be easier to manage and move around your greenhouse, but they will dry out quickly and need more regular watering. However, the temptation to plant into a very large container to reduce your workload should be balanced against the type of plant you're growing. Some vigorous plants like cucumbers, sweet potatoes, and tomatoes, for example, grow very quickly and are quite happy in a large container, whereas chilies and peppers can be overwhelmed in large volumes of cold potting mix, particularly in late spring.

There is no reason why vigorous plants cannot be sustained in smaller pots, but they will need more water and food to sustain healthy growth. Tomatoes and peppers, for example, can suffer with blossom end rot in summer, which is associated with erratic moisture levels. A larger volume of potting mix can help reduce this, thanks to the more consistent moisture levels it provides.

Types of containers

Pots come in all shapes and sizes and a range of materials, from terracotta to metal and plastic, offering a wealth of growing possibilities. You may need to balance practical and aesthetic considerations when choosing pots. The size and material will have a bearing on its weight and therefore how easy it is to move. Plastics, for example, are much lighter than terracotta, but terracotta is the more stylish option (see page 61 for more on terracotta versus plastic pots).

Grow bags have been used for crops such as tomatoes and cucumbers for many years in greenhouses. There are several available that contain peat-free growing media, which work very well. A standard grow bag will support two or three plants. Before planting, relieve any compaction that might hinder root growth by punching the sides of the bag. The disposable nature of single-use bags can be overcome by buying larger, reusable ones instead. Made of hard-wearing plastic, these will last for a number of years, and the greater volume of potting mix keeps plants moist for longer. The potting mix to fill reusable grow bags will obviously need to be sourced separately.

Hanging baskets make great use of the roof space within your greenhouse. Herbs, strawberries, and tumbling tomatoes are perfect plants to grow in your baskets, but you need to be conscious of the extra watering required when growing plants in baskets due to the small volume of potting mix and the free-draining nature of the liner.

Hanging baskets make full use of the roof space, providing beautiful floral displays or a safe haven for trailing strawberries.

Drainage: to crock or not?

Whether or not to use crocks has become a pretty contentious issue in recent years. It used to be standard practice to include a layer of broken terracotta, polystyrene, or stones at the base of your container for added drainage, but with most peat-free media, which drain freely, there is no need. There is also a school of thought that says a layer of crocks may harbor pests, such as slugs and snails, which can be detrimental to your plants.

For some plants, however (such as cacti, succulents, citrus, and stone fruit), drainage is crucial; they can suffer badly if there is an excessive amount of moisture in their root balls, particularly during winter. In these instances, that extra layer of crocks at the bottom may make all the difference in successfully overwintering your arid plants.

Of course, regardless of drainage, one reason why you might want to use crocks is because some containers have excessively large drainage holes through which potting mix can escape. A few well-placed larger pieces of terracotta or stones over these holes can help prevent this.

Growing media for containers

I grow a wide range of plants in containers under glass, from ferns to cacti, tropical plants, and many fruits and vegetables, all of which flourish in peat-free potting mix. Use this as the base for all your greenhouse container growing and you can't go far wrong. Extra drainage can be added if need be by mixing in a few handfuls of sand. And for plants that require very sharp drainage, such as cacti, a 50:50 mix of potting mix and sand is suitable.

Feeding

Most bagged peat-free potting mix will have enough nutrition to sustain container plants for between four and six weeks; beyond that, they will need a supplementary feed to get the best from them.

Containerized plants respond very quickly to liquid fertilizers. Between May and October, a weekly application will keep them in good health. Bear in mind that different fertilizers will provoke varied responses. A seaweed-based food will encourage gentle growth at the root and across the stems and leaves. A liquid nitrogen fertilizer will encourage strong, leafy growth, which is particularly useful as the plant matures and grows a framework for carrying flowers or fruit. A weekly potash feed will help sustain flowers and fruit and is best implemented when the plant is a reasonable size.

Topdressing

Topdressing with a layer of sand can be purely decorative, but also suppresses weeds and protects plant growth from being splashed with soil when watered. A topdressing of granular fertilizer, however, which is then lightly incorporated into the top few centimeters of the root ball, can increase the vigor of plants grown in containers for more than one season. The most effective will be a controlled-release feed that sustains the plant for a number of months. This can then be supplemented with a liquid feed to promote a certain type of growth.

Mulching

Adding a layer of fresh compost or composted bark to your container as a mulch will help retain moisture and suppress weeds. Although not overly attractive, cardboard will achieve the same result. Organic mulches will break down over time and need to be replaced to maintain their effectiveness.

Topdressing pots with a layer of sand reduces weeds and keeps shoots looking neat.

Repotting

When a plant breaks into active growth and shows signs of outgrowing its current container, this is when you should look to repot, as it will need more nutrition and extra rooting space. A restricted root run will provoke a stress response, such as flowering, which can be advantageous when growing plants like orchids, nerines, and African violets. But young plants that need to develop strong stems should be repotted regularly to maintain growth momentum and prevent premature flowering on inferior-sized plants. Repotting can be quite a brutal process, often damaging the roots and leading to a degree of stress for the plant. Just like when we prune the top growth of a plant, those wounds need to heal for fresh growth to be triggered.

Ideally, repotting should take place during the start of your plant's active growing period, when fresh foliage is being produced, because then the sap is moving through your plant, which will help repair damage and promote root growth. Plants that are repotted during winter or a dormant period do not have the same ability to recover from any root disturbance, which can lead to rotting and further damage to the root system. As the plant is not growing much during dormancy, there is no great need to repot it to sustain fresh growth.

Container hygiene

Plastic trays and pots, as well as terracotta containers, can be reused repeatedly. After each use, remove any potting mix from inside with a brush. Once all loose debris has been cleared from the container, wash it inside and out with warm, soapy water. Pay particular attention to the rim of a pot, which can harbor pests. Once your containers are thoroughly clean, dry them out in your greenhouse or outside on a still day before stacking them, ready to be reused.

Signs a plant needs repotting

- Lack of vigor.
- Roots appearing through the drainage holes of the pot.
- A tendency to dry out more regularly.

When roots are bursting through the drainage holes, it's time to repot your plant.

How to repot

Follow these steps to repot plants at the start of their active growth period.

01
Inspect your plant for signs that it needs repotting, such as roots circling inside the pot or poking through the drainage holes at the base.

02
Fill the base of a new, larger pot with peat-free potting mix, enough to bring the surface of the root ball to just below the top.

03
If the roots are congested, tease the outer roots away to improve the plant's establishment in the new container.

04
Place the plant in the center of the new pot and backfill around the root ball with potting mix.

05
Firm in the potting mix around the root ball to avoid any air gaps that will hinder root growth.

06
Water thoroughly to saturate the potting mix, encouraging roots to penetrate the fresh potting mix throughout the new pot.

Homemade nettle and comfrey fertilizers

The plants we cultivate in our greenhouses are totally dependent on us for water and extra nutrition outside of the small amount that exists in the potting mix. When choosing what kind of fertilizer you wish to use to give your plants a helping hand, it pays to go organic and make your own.

Any plant grower has a decision to make regarding the kind of fertilizer they choose to use to help promote healthy growth and assist their plants in the production of fruit and flowers. Synthetic fertilizers are man-made and have differing amounts of the major nutrients to directly benefit plant growth. These inorganic products have their place, but there are ethical questions surrounding their use (not to mention the cost) to consider. Excess synthetic nutrients in the soil can be detrimental to wildlife. So producing our own fertilizers through organic methods is more sustainable, more affordable, and more sympathetic to the environment and local wildlife.

Making your own nettle and comfrey fertilizers helps grow healthy and productive plants and is an easily achievable investment. Most of us have access to nettles and comfrey, either in the local surroundings or by finding a fertile spot in our gardens to grow them. The regular use of these organic fertilizers has produced very pleasing results in my plants, and I will continue to use them with a clear conscience.

“Producing our own fertilizers is more sustainable and affordable.”

Organic fertilizers

When we feed our plants, we need to consider which major nutrient to give in greater quantities to trigger different responses from our plants.

Nettle fertilizer

Nettle fertilizer is rich in nitrogen and supported by other minerals, helping promote strong, leafy growth. This type of fertilizer is particularly beneficial for developing plants and those where we want to encourage a strong framework to then support flowers and fruits. I tend to use nettle fertilizer once plants have been potted on from cuttings or moved into slightly larger pots from seedlings all the way through until the middle of the summer, when the emphasis tends to change more toward fruit and flowers.

Comfrey fertilizers

Comfrey tends to have a higher potash content, along with beneficial minerals, which helps promote more flowers and fruit. Comfrey fertilizer can be used from the middle of the summer to the end of the growing season, when all annual crops have finished. If growing comfrey in the garden, instead of foraging for it in the wild, be warned that it can self-seed prolifically; 'Bocking 14' is a sterile form that does not reproduce itself and is best suited to gardens.

Make your own fertilizers

There are many ways to make your own nettle and comfrey fertilizers, but this method works well for a standard garden. The general rule is to dilute your fertilizer one part concentrate to nine parts water, so in a 2-gallon (10-liter) watering can, you would use 1¾ pints (1 liter) of fertilizer concentrate and 2 gallons (9 liters) of water. I would suggest feeding your plants with this fertilizer once a week.

Instructions

Getting started

Place a 22-gallon (100-liter) rain barrel close to your greenhouse for convenience, as moving back and forth between your greenhouse and your fertilizer barrel will be a regular occurrence.

01

02

03

04

01

Fill an old pillowcase with nettles or comfrey, pushing the foliage down into the pillowcase so it is densely packed with plant material. Particularly in the case of nettles, make sure you wear thick gloves to avoid being stung. Place a large rock or a house brick in the pillowcase to help the bag of foliage sink to the base of the rain barrel.

02

Tie a knot in the top of the pillowcase and attach a length of wire below the knot that will then come out of the top of the rain barrel, enabling you to access the pillowcase when needed.

03

Lower the sealed pillowcase into the barrel. Make sure the wire remains on the outside of the barrel so the pillowcase can be removed easily when needed.

04

Fill the barrel with collected rainwater and allow to steep for three to four weeks before you begin to use your fertilizer. Once you have emptied the rain barrel of concentrate, repeat the process with more of the same plant or switch to a different type of organic fertilizer, depending on the time of year.

Allow a small area of nettles to grow in your garden. This will provide all you need for fertilizer and benefit wildlife, too.

How to grow in raised beds

Combining some of the key benefits of growing in containers and growing directly in the ground, nurturing plants in raised beds in your greenhouse can result in many gardening success stories.

The greater soil volume of raised beds offers plants a deeper root run than standard containers.

Whether you buy them premade or build your own (see page 86), raised beds are easy to construct in a medium to large greenhouse and are accessible, free-standing structures that you can move around the environment to suit different times of year and the crops you intend to grow.

Their generous size offers plants a deeper root run than standard containers, as well as the more consistent moisture levels that come with a greater volume of compost. They can also give you more control over the growing medium than growing in the ground, as it can be easily manipulated to improve conditions.

Aspect

Just as every effort should be made to position your greenhouse in full sun, as most fruits and vegetables will benefit from that sunny aspect, so raised beds should be positioned in full sun and ideally oriented from north to south for even light distribution. Sometimes, practicalities may necessitate a slight compromise, but it's best to choose the sunniest spot possible.

Dimensions

The length of your bed will be determined by the size of your greenhouse and your need to move in and around the structure. Bear in mind that beds of great length can be difficult to manage, being less mobile than shorter ones. The width of the bed is most important and should not exceed 4ft (1.2m). You need to be able to access the center from the side without having to kneel or step on the soil, which causes compaction as well as difficulties when stepping off again.

How to fill the bed

The soil in a raised bed should be fertile and free-draining. I find that green-waste compost is easy to get a hold of and extremely fertile, making it suitable for growing most crops. An ideal mix would be 50 percent garden compost, 40 percent topsoil,

The elevated height of raised beds makes them ideal for trailing cherry tomatoes.

Add compost to your growing medium for maximum fertility and top up as necessary.

and 10 percent sharp sand. The practicalities of mixing this growing medium can be difficult for some gardeners, in which case, filling your raised bed with well-rotted compost will suffice, but make sure it has lost all its heat, as otherwise it may scorch young plants. You may also find that this medium settles as it breaks down and needs topping up when crops are harvested.

What to grow

The advantage of having raised beds in your greenhouse is the greater flexibility to grow a range of plants in the generous extra space, including vegetables and cut flowers, which will benefit from the warmth and protection. You can even use them as a nursery bed for young plants and seedlings.

During early spring, when soil temperatures are cold, the extra warmth from the elevated bed provides a more conducive environment for young plants like salad leaves and herbs, encouraging them to grow more rapidly than they would if they were in the ground.

In the summer, raised beds are ideal for sowing cut flowers, such as zinnias, in drills (see page 203) or for growing sprawling climbers or tumblers, such as peppers, sweet potatoes, trailing strawberries, and tomatoes. The circumscribed nature of raised beds also makes them perfect for organizing crops on a rotational system.

Build a raised bed

Raised beds are well worth considering when planning your greenhouse. They facilitate growing larger plants and those with deeper roots and the seasonal rotation of crops with more permanency. They are especially useful for gardeners with limited mobility or for those who do not relish the thought of dragging bags of compost and pots in and out of a greenhouse each season.

Raised beds will provide a deeper rooting zone for your plants, meaning they will dry out less frequently, compared to using grow bags or pots. Raised beds also enable you to garden at a more comfortable height, and building your own means you can tailor it to suit your needs.

There is no need to replace the entirety of the compost in a raised bed each year. Simply replace the top 20 percent each spring. Coupled with a seasonal feeding regime, this will give great results and save you money on compost, too.

Build your raised bed in your greenhouse (if space allows) so you don't have to carry this potentially cumbersome structure too far.

Additional benefits to growing plants in a raised bed within your greenhouse include the following:

- Soil temperatures within a raised bed tend to be higher than the open soil, meaning earlier harvests and sowings during the spring and an extended growing season in the fall.
- Growing plants at height protects them from being damaged by human traffic or wheelbarrows.
- Raised beds contain the soil and keep the greenhouse environment tidy with minimal compost on pathways and floors.
- Elevated plants are kept out of reach from pests, such as rabbits.
- For gardens with poor soils, raised beds offer an opportunity to create a more fertile rooting zone with improved drainage. Good-quality topsoil mixed with well-rotted manure or compost will create a healthy growing media.

Basic construction

Decide on the dimensions you want for your raised bed, considering access and movement around your greenhouse. The measurements below for my raised bed were dictated by the size of my space and the height of five stacked horizontal slats.

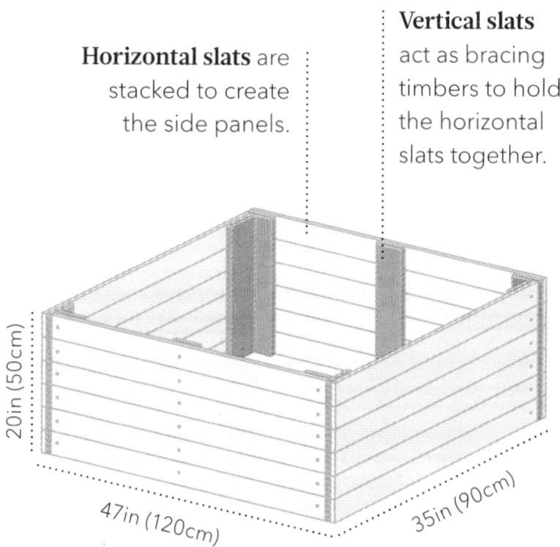

“Raised beds will provide a deeper rooting zone for your plants and enable you to garden at a more comfortable height.”

Wooden pallet collars can be easily stacked to create a cheap and effective raised bed.

Budget-friendly beds

Raised beds can be bought premade, of course, but they can also be constructed using recycled or reclaimed materials, offering a cheaper and more versatile alternative.

Interlocking wooden pallet collars are widely available online and easy to set up as raised beds by simply stacking the collars vertically so that each one sits within the metal corner brackets of the one below (see image above right). Two or three collars high will give a versatile and easily relocated bed.

For this DIY raised-bed project, however, I have used recycled pallet wood, allowing me to create a size that fits my space.

Equipment

2–3 wooden pallets (with slats of the same width for uniformity in height)

Tools to disassemble the pallets (large flat-headed screwdriver and claw hammer, crowbar, or pallet breaker)

Tape measure

Pencil

Wood saw

Screws (enough to secure each slat at each corner and the bracing timbers)

Screwdriver (preferably electric)

Large triangle

Level

Green-waste compost or bagged peat-free potting mix, or a 50:50 mix of quality topsoil and green-waste compost

Instructions

01
Disassemble the pallets, using a large flat-headed screwdriver and claw hammer to pry the slats from the frame. Knock out any existing nails and reuse if suitable. Try to preserve as much timber as possible. Measure and saw the horizontal slats for the sides and two shorter ends.

02
Cut three vertical bracing timbers for each side panel from the spare pallet wood at a length equivalent to the ultimate height of the bed.

03
Screw the horizontal slats to the vertical bracing timbers to create solid front and back panels. Ensure the bracing timbers are attached on the inside of the panels for a neater finish. Use a triangle and level to prevent the angles of your panels from becoming distorted.

04
Construct the two sides of your bed in the same way. I found that the shorter sides only required a bracing timber at each end. Position the side and end panels to form the rectangular bed.

01

02

04

03

05
Attach the sides together at the corners, screwing through the bracing timbers at each end of the panels.

06
My raised bed was positioned on slabs with gaps between them, allowing the water to drain away. If your bed is on a nonporous surface, meaning drainage will be compromised, add a layer of rubble to the bottom of the bed to allow surplus moisture to drain from the soil, preventing waterlogging, which will be detrimental to healthy growth. Lining the inside of your bed with landscape fabric is an option to extend the life of the timber, but this will add to the cost of the project. Last of all, fill the bed with green-waste compost or a 50:50 mixture of green-waste compost and topsoil. If you intend to sow directly into your bed, allow for the top 2in (5cm) to be filled with peat-free potting mix.

05

06

A space for propagation

It's all too easy to rely on garden centers to provide us with the instant gratification of fully grown plants. But for cost-effectiveness and pure satisfaction, nothing can beat propagating from either seed or flourishing plant. This is where greenhouses come into their own.

Regardless of how long I've been propagating plants, the sheer joy and wonder I get from seeing freshly emerging seedlings or new growth on a rooted cutting never subsides. It is always one of the highlights of my gardening year. Garden centers and nurseries are incredibly good at producing young plants, which can save us a lot of time, but it should not detract from the pure satisfaction we can get from propagating plants at home.

Plants can be propagated in a number of ways, and the varying techniques offer different outcomes. In this section, we will explore the main propagation techniques of raising plants from seed, cuttings, and division. Growing from seed often results in high numbers of plants, but genetically those seedlings will all vary slightly. Cuttings or division, on the other hand, give a replica of the parent plant, offering uniformity in the new crop. Sometimes, in a garden, consistency or repetition is desired; at other times, variability can be incredibly attractive.

Starting off your seedlings or new shoots in a greenhouse will give far better results than growing them outside, as you can protect these young, vulnerable plants from cold, wet, and windy weather while increasing the air temperature to accelerate growth. They can then be hardened off ready for the garden or grown to a size that can be potted on for the greenhouse. Growing on young plants under cover also makes it easier to protect them from pests, allowing them to grow strong and relatively large—and therefore more resilient to pest damage—before planting outside.

Growing plants from seeds, cuttings, or division means that we can produce much larger quantities, and often the choice of what we can grow is far greater than fully grown plants. Seeds in particular can open up all sorts of possibilities for growing rare and unusual plants that you just won't find online or in garden centers and nurseries.

Growing from seed offers a huge number of plants, as well as unusual species.

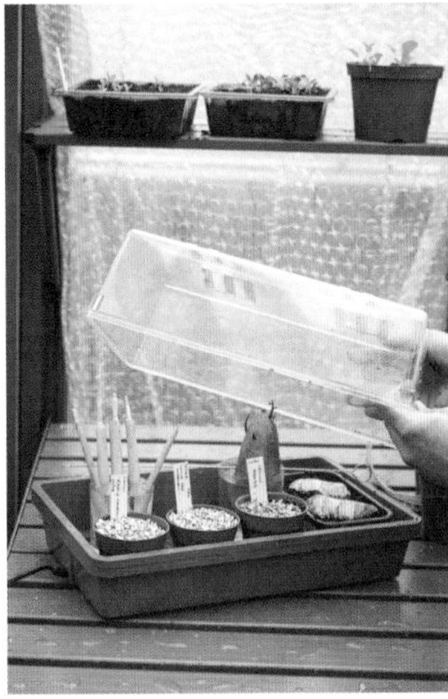

A heated propagator is an invaluable tool for seed germination, as well as encouraging rooted cuttings, such as lemongrass, sweet potato, and ginger.

A greenhouse is ideal for growing on all types of propagated plants, whether from seed, cuttings, or division.

Types of propagation

Seeds

- Inexpensive.
- Easy to obtain and collect.
- Produces a high number of plants.
- Natural variation has a decorative quality.

Cuttings

- Replicates the parent plant's habit and characteristics.
- Ideal when seed is expensive or not easily obtainable.
- Useful when only a few plants are required.

Division

- One of the easiest methods, with a high success rate.
- A straightforward way to increase plant numbers.
- Replicates the parent plant's habit and characteristics.

Propagation techniques: from seed

One of the most economical and plentiful ways to grow plants is from seed, and a greenhouse is the perfect place to do it. This section covers the entire process, from sowing to potting on a young plant.

Growing from seed can provide a large number of plants, though they will not necessarily be identical. If you were to collect seeds from a sunflower, for example, and sow them the following year, there would be shared characteristics but a degree of variability within the offspring.

Plants are very sophisticated, and when growing from seed, often all that is required from gardeners is a gentle helping hand to provide the conditions they will thrive in. Often, almost everything a seed needs is already in place within the seed itself. By providing them with a degree of moisture and the correct temperature, you will trigger the first root to initiate and start growing into the soil to absorb water and nutrients. Once that root has started to develop, a new shoot will start growing up toward the light, producing seed leaves followed by the first set of true leaves, which are indicative of the plant. This is where labeling is crucial because many seedlings can look almost identical at first.

Generally, greenhouse plants that thrive in the summer, such as tomatoes, chilies, and eggplants, will require warmer temperatures to germinate than hardier plants, such as sweet peas and cabbages.

Different seeds may require varying treatments to grow, so always check your seed packet for individual instructions. As a general rule of thumb, however, the following method for sowing seeds can be applied to most plants.

Store leftover seeds in a cool, dry place to stop them from drying out. Resealing packets with adhesive tape can help retain moisture and increase the lifespan and viability of your seeds.

Grown from seed in February, *Antirrhinum majus* 'Ruby' gives tall cut flowers all summer.

Instructions

01
Fill your seed pan or tray with peat-free potting mix, removing any large lumps by rubbing the mix between your palms. Fine seed may require the potting mix to be sieved to achieve more uniform germination. Level the mix with the top of your pot or with your hand.

02
If using a cell tray, use two fingers to firm the potting mix within each cell. Otherwise, use a tamper or the base of another pot to firm and level the surface, creating a gap of around ½in (1cm) from the top of the pot or tray, allowing space for the seeds and a light covering of potting mix or vermiculite.

03
Water the firmed potting mix with a small watering can to saturate it. Remember to use tap water to avoid the risk of bacteria and disease affecting your seedlings. By saturating the potting mix, the seeds should have enough moisture to trigger germination without the need to water them again in the first week or so.

04
For cell trays, place two or three seeds in each cell with the ambition of selecting one seedling later. For seed trays, sow your seeds sparsely over the firm, moist surface, ensuring they are distributed around the edges, as well as the center.

05
Label and date your seeds, then cover lightly with sieved potting mix or vermiculite. Larger seeds can often be covered completely; some seeds may need to be barely covered, and some may not need cover at all. Check the seed packet to see if light is required to help germination. If you're unsure, generally the finer the seed, the less covering it needs.

01

02

03

04

05

Pricking out seedlings into their own cell gives them the space and nutrition to develop strong roots.

Pricking out

We help a seedling develop by increasing the volume and nutrition of medium it is growing in through a process called "pricking out," which involves transplanting a young seedling into a larger cell or pot. If left, seedlings will develop their root systems and become intertwined. By transplanting and placing them in their own volume of general-purpose potting mix, which provides greater nutrition than seed-starting mix, you will allow them to develop a root system without competition.

Tips

- Label, label, label—most seedlings will look very similar, so don't trust your memory. Write a label for every tray, or every plant if varieties are mixed.
- Avoid exposing pricked-out seedlings to potentially fatal heat right away. Place them in a cool spot in dappled light for the first 12 hours and then in your greenhouse once they have stabilized.
- You can avoid the process of pricking out and save time by sowing a few seeds directly into a cell tray. Reduce the group of seedlings to one strong seedling by removing the weaker seedlings with a pair of scissors at the base. This will allow the single strongest seedling to develop and fill the cell.

Instructions

01
First, water the potting mix in the pots or cell tray you are transferring your seedlings to with a small watering can to avoid too much disturbance. Alternatively, you can water the seedlings after pricking out by placing the pots in a water bath to absorb the moisture from below. It will probably take half an hour or so for the potting mix to reach the point of saturation.

02
Transfer your seedlings individually, when they have developed their first set of true leaves, which follow the first set of leaves, often known as the seed leaves. (Most seedlings look similar at the seed-leaf stage; it is only when the true leaves emerge that the characteristics of the leaf are revealed.) Hold them by a seed leaf to avoid damaging the fragile stem and true leaves or exposing them to your warm, oily fingers. Tease the roots away from the medium with a skewer or pricking-out tool, lifting the seedling and its root system clear of the seed tray or pot.

03
Create a hole in the center of the cell or small pot of growing mix you are transferring to; the hole should be deeper and wider than the root of your seedling to enable you to lower the roots into it without causing damage. Leggy seedlings can be planted a little deeper, up to the base of the seed leaf, to improve the stability of the plant and help produce more robust growth in the weeks to come.

04
Backfill the hole with your skewer or pricking-out tool, keeping a hold of that seed leaf, then releasing your grip once the seedling is stable and firmed in.

Choose your moment.
It's best not to prick out seedlings on a very warm day, as this can cause them to wilt.

Potting on

Transferring young plants into larger pots after they have established in cell trays or small pots is known as "potting on" or "potting up." It is best to pot on gradually into a pot that's no more than double the size of the original. Although some vigorous plants will be able to accommodate a huge leap from a small pot to a large one, most will have their growth checked by coming into contact with a large volume of cold, wet potting mix. They would probably recover in time, but if you compared a plant that was potted on regularly into a slightly larger pot with one that had gone from a very small pot into one 10 times the size, the first plant would be larger with a stronger root system. What we feel may save us time often leads to an inferior plant in the long run, so it's a good idea to pot on gradually to keep that growth rate constant. The instructions below show potting on cuttings, but the method is the same for seedlings.

Instructions

01

Identify the larger pot that you wish to use, avoiding a leap in size that is more than double the original pot. Ensure that there are adequate drainage holes at the base. Remove the plant from its original pot.

02

With your fingers, gently tease out the roots at the base of the seedling to help them establish in the new potting mix. Remove the first centimeter or half-inch of the mix from the top of the root ball to allow space for fresh potting mix and to remove any dormant weed seeds or moss.

03

Put a couple small handfuls of potting mix in the base of the new container and place the root ball of the seedling on top, adding or removing potting mix until the root ball is at the correct height. It should sit a little below the top of the pot so there is enough room for the water to pool around the plant; this is known as a watering gap.

04

Once your root ball is positioned, fill around the sides with potting mix, firming with your fingers and making sure there are no air pockets and that the pot is full.

01

02

03

04

05

Roots will not grow in an air gap, so avoid these by taking some time to make sure that medium fills the entire pot around the root ball.

05
Level off the potting mix with your hands, maintaining that watering gap, then water the plant thoroughly. Rewater when the plant begins to dry out. The best way to gauge this is by pushing your fingers into the potting mix: If it feels dry below the surface, you should add some moisture. Be conscious that peat-free potting mixes may appear dry on the surface but often hold a lot of moisture below.

Troubleshooting issues growing plants from seed

- Timing is everything. Don't be tempted to sow your seeds too early, as the cold temperatures and lower light levels will make germination slow and cause your seedlings to be leggy and weak. Later sowings will soon catch up with those that have been sown a few weeks earlier.
- Some seeds benefit from being covered with a pane of glass or a seed tray lid or placed in a plastic bag to retain humidity, until a good level of germination has been achieved. Remove the glass/lid/bag once seeds have germinated to prevent rot and to harden up the seedlings.
- Think about when you want to plant out. Bedding plants and other tender plants often need to be protected until the risk of frost has passed, so wait until March and April at the earliest to start them off. There is no merit in having large tomato plants in March (without sophisticated heating and lighting systems).
- Overcrowded seedlings at any stage will result in drawn and leggy plants. Sow seeds thinly, prick out in good time, and space young plants out when they become congested.
- Be patient and harden off young plants before they go out into the garden (see page 27). Expose young plants to cooler temperatures during the day and bring them in at night, then gradually expose them to nighttime temperatures over several days or a week. Consider when you wish to plant out and begin to harden them off a week or two before then. Many plants are not frost-hardy, and usually by the end of May that risk has gone, so hardening off tender plants in the second half of May will mean they are garden-ready come the end of the month.
- Damping off is caused by watering vulnerable seedlings from above, which can lead to a fungal disease that kills them off. Increase air circulation, reduce the temperature, prick out, and water from below to avoid issues.

Propagation techniques: cuttings

Growing plants from cuttings means that you produce a replica of the plant you're taking a cutting from, as opposed to growing from seed, which will produce more diversity among the plants you grow. So if you want exact multiples of some of your favorite plants at almost no cost, then taking cuttings is the propagation method for you.

Plants propagated from cuttings will inherit all the attributes of the parent plant. For example, if you propagated a yellow-flowered dahlia from cuttings, it would be highly likely that all those young plants would also produce yellow flowers. If you collected seed from that same dahlia, you would most probably get several seedlings that produced a yellow flower, but there would also be a number with flowers of different colors. Producing plants from seed will give you much greater numbers of plants with different characteristics, but by propagating plants from cuttings or vegetatively, you ensure that the characteristics of the new plants are the same as the parent.

Types of cuttings

The plant and the time of year will dictate the type of cutting you take for the best chance of success. The most common type of cutting is from a stem, but it is also possible to grow plants from leaves and roots. This is because shoots, roots, and leaves of certain plants have a concentration of meristems–unspecialized stem cells that can divide and become any type of cell. By harnessing these meristems, we can propagate from different parts of our plants, generating root cells that can then support plant growth. Roots cut from dormant parent plants can therefore establish their own root system, while leaf cuttings can produce new plants where their veins come into contact with growing medium.

When we take a stem cutting, we often trim just below a bud or node and remove the lower leaves. The wound that is created at the base then begins to callus, and new roots (known as adventitious roots) emerge. Material can be taken as "basal" cuttings, which simply means severing a section of stem from initial growth that emerges from the soil or base of the parent plant. This material is often soft and pliable; dahlias, chrysanthemums, and

Soft, new growth sprouting from the base of the plant is the ideal material for softwood cuttings.

By taking cuttings, you can multiply your plants for free. Pelargoniums, chrysanthemums, and dahlias can all be propagated easily this way.

delphiniums are often propagated this way. "Nodal" cuttings are taken from a section of stem with a node or leaf joint at the base and a bud or leaf joint at the tip. Nodes are places in the stem where increased concentrations of hormones accumulate, which encourages callusing and root initiation.

Growing medium

Cuttings don't require any nutrition to initiate roots. They do, however, require good air circulation and drainage from their potting mix. The best medium for rooting cuttings is peat-free potting mix mixed with perlite or sand, for drainage, at a 50:50 ratio. Once you see roots appearing through the holes at the bottom of the pot, it is a surefire sign to pot on your cuttings into a peat-free potting mix and start a feeding regime of seaweed fertilizer once a week to help the plant bulk up.

Take more cuttings than you need, as surplus specimens can always be given away to friends and neighbors.

Aftercare

Without roots, cuttings have no means to absorb moisture, therefore the environment in which we keep them needs to have high humidity to maintain their health and buoyancy. Placing your pot of cuttings in a clear plastic bag will maintain relative humidity and protect them from drying out. This is the simplest way of rooting cuttings, but a windowsill propagator with a gentle base heat will create slightly more favorable conditions. Mist your cuttings with water every day to hydrate them. Water the potting mix once a week or more regularly if necessary to prevent it from drying out.

Make sure that your cuttings are well rooted before you remove them from your propagator or the plastic bag. Fresh growth on the cutting is often a good sign that roots are developing, but this isn't always the case. Resist the temptation to pull at your cuttings, as this will hinder root development;

Transfer cuttings such as dahlias (top) and fuchsias (above) to individual pots when strong roots have developed, then water in well.

Tips

- **Provide initial shade** When you first take your cuttings, they are very vulnerable, and a warm greenhouse with bright light can be very damaging and kill them off. Once you've taken your cuttings, sit the container in a saucer of water and place either under your staging or in the shade for 48 hours to allow them to rehydrate before moving them into more dappled conditions. Avoid intense light at this stage, as this may damage your cuttings before they have produced roots and are more capable of coping with extreme conditions.
- **Encourage branching** If you intend to grow a standard fuchsia or coleus, then encouraging a single stem is an important part of the process (see page 209). However, for most other cuttings, we want healthy branching, so, once rooted, gently remove the tip of the cutting to encourage strong side shoots and a well-developed plant.

instead, look out for those young white roots peering out of the drainage holes at the base of the pot, which is a clear sign that your cuttings are ready to pot on.

Acclimatize your cuttings to the greenhouse environment over a few days in their original container before you pot them on. This means allowing the plant to adapt to lower humidity levels and higher light levels than they're used to. For example, to begin with, remove the lid of a propagator or open the plastic bag to allow your plants to become accustomed to the conditions within the main body of your greenhouse during the day. After a few days, leave the lid/bag off at night for another few days before repotting. Plants will not need to be returned to the propagator beyond that point and can be gradually hardened off (see page 27) before moving outside.

Humidity is needed for most cuttings to establish roots. If you don't have a propagator, simply use a clear plastic bag instead.

Pelargonium cuttings, once potted on and fully established, can be hardened off in a cold frame.

Fuchsia sides shoots (above) can be rooted easily in a glass of water. Refresh the water every other day to prevent bacteria build-up.

Young dahlia shoots (left) provide the ideal material for taking softwood basal cuttings in early summer.

Stem cuttings

Stem cuttings are often categorized by the time of year that we take them or the level of maturity of the stem. Young growth is often described as **softwood**, and propagation usually takes place in the early summer. **Semi-ripe** wood cuttings are taken in late summer, when the stem tissue is generally a bit firmer and woodier. **Hardwood** cuttings are taken at the end of the growing season and into fall, when the stems are fully ripened and woody.

Softwood cuttings are made of the tips of nonflowering stems or young basal shoots, which generally root quickly and are often a way to root difficult-to-propagate plants. Chrysanthemums and dahlias are great examples of softwood or basal cuttings but need a supportive environment to root, with extra humidity, as the plant material is at its most vulnerable.

Semi-ripe cuttings have a more robust nature than softwood cuttings, as they are firmer and more mature. Pelargoniums, heliotropes, and fuchsias are examples of greenhouse plants that should be propagated by this method.

Hardwood cuttings or ripe wood cuttings are the most robust and easy to nurture. Hardwood cuttings can fall into two categories: those with and without leaves. Evergreen plants, such as hollies and rhododendrons, can be propagated this way, as well as deciduous plants, such as roses, dogwoods, and willows.

Taking semi-ripe wood cuttings from a pelargonium

These types of cuttings are suitable for most tender perennials that provide a riot of color throughout the summer, such as heliotropes, pelargoniums, and fuchsias. Semi-ripe wood cuttings can be taken from July until the end of September, when the stems have matured enough to be less pliable but not completely ripened and woody. This type of cutting has enough vitality within the stem to root quickly with the added benefit of maturity, which makes the material more robust to cope with slightly more extreme conditions compared to a softwood cutting.

Instructions

01

First, assemble your equipment: cutting implements (pruners, scissors, or a knife), small plant pot filled with gritty potting mix, skewer, small watering can, and propagator or clear plastic bag. Select a healthy, nonflowering shoot from the parent plant, around 2-4in (5-10cm) long. Sever the stem by cutting just above a leaf node, then remove the lower two-thirds of leaves from the stem.

02

Next, cut the base of the severed stem just below a leaf node.

03

Trim away the very tip of the cutting, which reduces the risk of wilting. Large-leaved cuttings should have their leaves cut in half to further reduce water loss.

04

Insert your cuttings into gritty, well-drained potting mix (see page 99) around the edge of the pot, using the skewer or a pencil as a dibble, then fill in at a depth that leaves the top third of the stem exposed. Don't worry if the cuttings are slightly crowded. This will help increase humidity, which will aid rooting.

05

Water the cuttings generously to saturate the potting mix and place in a position out of direct sunlight in a propagator or inside a clear plastic bag that is folded underneath the pot to seal it and trap moisture. Do not allow the potting mix to dry out and keep the humidity within the bag or propagator high until fresh roots appear through the drainage holes at the base of the pot. This indicates that the cuttings are ready to be potted on.

01

02

03

04

05

Cuttings lose water easily. Have all your equipment ready before you start so you can pot up and water them quickly.

Leaf cuttings

Leaf cuttings can be a lot of fun to try. In this technique, sections or whole leaves are taken as cuttings and inserted into potting mix, where plantlets form where the surface of the potting mix meets the leaf veins. Streptocarpus, begonias, African violets, and peperomia are propagated by this method.

Taking leaf cuttings from a streptocarpus

These plants generally require quite specific greenhouse environments, needing both humidity and protection from extreme sun to root, but they make great houseplants.

Instructions

01
Take a mature leaf from the parent plant, removing it with pruners as low as possible.

02
On a chopping board, turn the leaf upside down to reveal the underside and the main midrib. Cut along each side of the midrib with a sharp knife to reveal the leaf veins within.

03
Create two shallow trenches with your hand in a seed tray containing peat-free potting mix mixed with 50 percent sand or perlite. Then insert the two sections of leaf.

04
Gently firm the leaf sections into the potting mix and water well. Place in a heated propagator or a plastic bag on a well-lit windowsill but away from direct and scorching heat. Young plants will appear where the leaf veins meet the potting mix in around 10–12 weeks.

01

02

03

04

Root cuttings

Herbaceous perennials, such as phlox, poppies, anemones, and acanthus, can be propagated using this method, which involves lifting the plant in the fall or late winter when it is dormant.

To protect the parent plant and ensure that it establishes well when replanted in the garden, only remove one-third of the root ball for cuttings.

Taking root cuttings from acanthus

No extra heat or humidity is needed with these cuttings, as warmth encourages them to shoot without a reasonable root system to support new growth. In winter and early spring, these cuttings will grow steadily and slowly in an unheated greenhouse or cold frame, producing leaves when the roots below can support growth.

Instructions

01
Wash the root ball of the plant, then select a young, vigorous root that is around pencil thickness and cut it off near the crown with a sharp knife.

02
Cut the root into lengths of around 2-4in (5-10cm); a few cuttings may be achievable from one root. Make sure you remember which is the top of the cutting (nearest the crown of the plant) and which is the bottom (farthest from the crown).

03
Insert the cuttings vertically into some peat-free potting mix mixed with 50 percent sand or perlite for extra drainage, with the top of the cutting just below the surface. Remember to label the pot.

04
Cover the surface of the potting mix with a layer of gravel to keep weed seeds from developing and to lock in moisture.

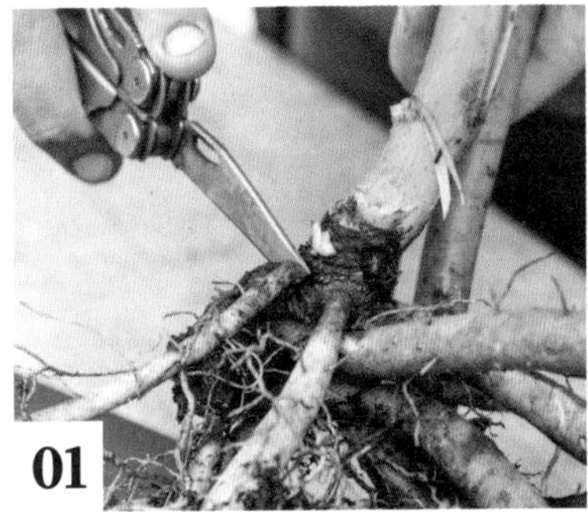

01

02

03

04

05
Water well and place in a cool environment, such as an unheated greenhouse or cold frame, until fresh growth appears the following spring. Look out for those fresh roots at the bottom of the pot before you consider potting on.

05

Propagation techniques: division

Division is the simplest form of propagation there is, and it's the ideal technique for plenty of perennials, as well as congested pots of supermarket herbs.

Dividing perennials is one of the easiest methods of propagation. Simply insert two forks into the clump back to back and pry apart.

Not only will division increase the number of plants in your garden, but the process has the benefit of rejuvenating the parent plant, which may have become less vigorous or congested over time. Sometimes, the center of a clump has rotted away as the plant spreads—this material can be composted, as we only want to retain the younger, more vigorous growth for a better performance in the garden or greenhouse.

When dividing herbaceous perennials, the smallest clump I would recommend is the size of a clenched fist, which will give you a reasonable plant in that first year. The size and thickness of the parent plant's root ball will dictate the type of tool or approach that you need for division. Some plants may be easily pulled apart with your hands, and others by inserting two hand forks back to back and prying them apart. The more fibrous and robust root balls will require a spade to split them; two border forks placed back to back and pried apart; or, in extreme cases, an old wood saw or ax.

Avoid dividing perennials when they are in full growth. The best time will be in the spring in most cases, just as the plants are waking up, are full of vigor, and have an entire growing season to establish in the garden. Some early flowering perennials, such as pulmonarias, epimediums, and hellebores, will benefit from a fall division, as the plants have time to establish and then provide flowers the following spring, although the performance may be modest in the first year.

Division is also ideal for propagating from supermarket herbs, as the pots often contain a multitude of seedlings or stems, which can be split. Not only will you increase your number of plants, but the process of division often makes them last longer, as it alleviates the congestion.

Perennials that can be easily divided

Aster	Hosta	Sedum
Astrantia	Nepeta	Trollius
Geranium	Pulmonaria	Veronica
Helenium	Rudbeckia	

Dividing supermarket herbs

Pots of supermarket herbs such as basil, parsley, mint, and cilantro can be easily divided and grown on as individual plants.

Instructions

01

Fill several new containers at least twice the size of the original with peat-free potting mix.

02

Carefully remove the root ball of the supermarket herbs from its original container.

03

Gently tease apart the roots to separate the root ball of the parent plant into several clumps.

04

Plant the separate new clumps of herbs into the new pots, firm in, and water well. When each new plant has established, they can be planted out into a raised bed in the greenhouse to grow on.

Watering: an overview

During active growth, it's best to saturate the potting mix and wait for the moisture to be used up before watering again.

The way we water our plants has the single greatest impact on how well they grow. Too much or too little water, or watering at the wrong time, can all be hugely damaging, and this is especially true when growing under glass.

In greenhouses, plants require constant attention. Container-grown plants especially depend on us for everything, water and good drainage being the ultimate imperatives. This may seem obvious, but our greenhouse plants are growing with no access to natural rainfall, so as gardeners we must intervene. We need to use our instincts and, by observing our plants and understanding what they need, learn the art of watering. It's a key skill to develop, because the signs plants give us are not always straightforward.

Watering in winter

One of the most common mistakes during the winter is killing plants through kindness by overwatering. Plants cannot process water when they're not actively growing. By watering too often, plants become saturated, as does the medium in the pot, leading to anaerobic conditions; this results in root damage and rot, which is often fatal.

It is far better to be conservative with watering during these more dormant months. If you are in any doubt, my advice would be to refrain from watering, as it is easier to revive a dry plant that may be wilting than it is to reinvigorate a sodden one. Insert your finger into the root ball; if moisture is present, it is unlikely that your plant needs watering at that time.

Watering in summer

In most cases, plants will require watering daily during the summer, when in full growth. At this time of year, a lack of moisture can lead to stunted and poor growth, but overwatering (particularly of young plants) is still a danger.

With many peat-free potting mixes, for example, the surface of the soil can feel and look dry, but by inserting your finger into the potting mix, you can often detect moisture–meaning that, despite appearances, the plant doesn't need watering. Similarly, during the summer, plants can suffer from heat stress, resulting in their leaves starting to wilt. But this is a little misleading, too, as it is often a sign of excessive temperatures, not a lack of water. By adding more water to root systems when it's not needed, we actually exacerbate the problem. The plant should recover quite naturally if ventilation is increased and the temperatures cool. So continue to check moisture levels within your pots and water only when necessary for healthy growth.

Plants generally don't require frequent dribbles of water, as this will encourage surface rooting and poor root development within the container or soil.

It is far more effective for the plants to be watered thoroughly to saturate the potting mix or soil during the active growing period, then left until the water has been used up by the plant before resaturating. This action will result in a much healthier plant with a deeper root system.

Utility vs. rainwater

If you live in an area with hard water or water with a high pH level, using utility water on plants may lead to nutrient deficiencies and calcium build-up on the surface of leaves. Rainwater will provide much softer water with a more neutral pH, which is less likely to harm the plants. It is also the more sustainable option. Particularly during the height of summer, our greenhouses can require a great deal of water on a daily basis, so to mitigate the environmental impact, we should harvest as much rainwater as is practically possible using rain barrels and tanks (see page 110).

The exception will be when you have exhausted your rainwater supply, or when plants are very young. Utility water is treated and therefore free from bacteria that can be harmful to young seedlings. Once they have been potted on into 2¾in (7cm) pots, however, they are robust enough to process some of the bacteria present in rainwater.

Avoid overwatering in winter by pushing your finger into the soil to test moisture levels. **In summer,** most plants, especially those in containers, will need watering every day.

Watering: water capture

Greenhouses need a lot of water to sustain the plants within them during the summer. Because it's such a precious resource, we need to collect water where we can and be as self-sufficient with its use as possible. Connecting water tanks and rain barrels to every available roof space and gutter is one of the most effective ways to be environmentally conscious as we garden under glass.

In an ideal world, we would only use utility water supplies to irrigate the seedlings and young plants in our greenhouse until they are robust enough to be watered with rainwater (see page 109) so that most of our irrigation needs are met by harvested rainwater. There is one snag, however: When it comes to harvesting rainwater, we tend to have a lot of water when we don't need it during the winter months—and then, at the height of summer, when we need to water our plants a lot more frequently, rainwater can be scarce.

The secret to success is to capture lots of rainwater in tanks and rain barrels during times of plenty. Though it might seem excessive to have several water tanks and barrels in your garden during the rainy months, you'll be surprised by how much water you'll go through during the growing season.

Installing a rain barrel

Evaluate the gutter systems of your home, garages, and sheds, as well as the potential rainwater harvesting capability of the roof of your greenhouse. If your greenhouse is built on a level base, then water should be evenly distributed between the four corners of the structure. In this case, a rain barrel or tank at each corner would be ideal. Harvesting rainwater from the roof of your house will provide a greater volume of water, but the aesthetics of having rain barrels and tanks around the home may not be to everyone's taste, so this is a personal choice and something to consider carefully. Rain barrels either come with your greenhouse kit or can be purchased online, along with the adapters needed to connect the gutters of your greenhouse to the tank or barrel.

Installing a rain barrel at each corner of your greenhouse will capture rainwater running off the roof.

Water tanks

Another option is to install an open water tank in your garden (connected to a downspout, fed from a gutter), either by purchasing one new or by repurposing an old, galvanized water tank. These tanks provide an easy-access solution to watering, as you can simply dunk your watering can into the water, which fills it much more quickly than a rain barrel. Given the many trips back and forth you are likely to make between the tank and your plants, this speedy efficiency can be very welcome.

An open water tank also has the added benefit of attracting and supporting wildlife, especially during times of low rainfall. When setting up an open water tank, make sure that you have a means by which wildlife can escape if they fall in–either a metal strip or weighted wooden plank to act as a ramp, which allows creatures to emerge from the water and escape to the edge or rim of the tank, avoiding drowning through fatigue. Mosquitoes can pose a problem with open water tanks, but this can easily be avoided by netting the top of the tank to prevent them from laying their eggs in the water.

Tip

Clean out your rain barrels and tanks at the end of the summer to prevent the water from becoming stagnant, which can lead to fungal and bacterial diseases that are potentially harmful to you or your plants.

An open water tank makes for easy access when filling a watering can; rain barrels can be connected directly to greenhouse gutters to capture run-off.

Watering techniques

Creating a depression in the soil around plants gives water direct access to the root ball.

As you get to know your greenhouse and the plants within it, you will establish a routine and develop a sensitivity to your plants' needs. And knowing what your different plants need will determine when and how you water them.

The best time to water your greenhouse plants is first thing in the morning; they then have the entire day to utilize that moisture to grow stems, leaves, fruits, flowers, and roots. As they go into evening, when temperatures fall, it is far healthier for the plant to be on the drier side than to have a sodden root ball. This is especially important in winter and early spring, when plants are vulnerable to rot.

If you have the choice to grow both in the ground and in containers, be aware that you will need to water container plants more regularly than those in the ground, as the latter have access to water and nutrition deeper in the soil. The benefit with container plants, however, is that we can allow moisture levels to fluctuate a little to encourage flowering. Some plants, such as *Streptocarpus* or citrus, respond to the stress of drying out slightly between waterings by producing flowers and seed to reproduce before conditions worsen. We can also keep container plants drier at the beginning and end of the growing season to avoid rot.

How to water

Plants mostly need water at the root ball, not all over the leaves or floor. Damping down can benefit certain plants that like humidity (see overleaf), but for many, wet foliage can lead to botrytis and rot. Leaves cannot absorb vast amounts of water, so wet leaves will often only lead to scorching and disease. By watering the root ball directly, your plant will recover quickly and make efficient use of the water. Freshly sown seeds and young seedlings with a delicate root system should be placed in a seed bath so they can absorb water from below to avoid disturbance and damping off. When establishing new plants in the ground, a good way to directly

Basic tools

Using a watering can is efficient, as the amount of water you apply can be easily controlled. A hose can save time, but it is harder to gauge how much water you are giving your plants. As an experiment, try holding the hose over a bucket for just a few seconds. You may be surprised at how much water you are applying to your plant when it is visualized in front of you.

target the root ball and prevent water from seeping away is to create a shallow, bowl-like depression around the base. This trench captures the water and directs it straight down toward the roots.

Mulching is also useful for locking in moisture by reducing evaporation. This has the added benefit of suppressing weed growth and adding extra fertility to the soil. Only mulch on moist, weed-free soil with a 2-4in (5-10cm) layer of material (compost, wood chips, or leaf mold, for example). The best times to apply it are immediately after planting and halfway through the growing season if compost levels have dropped and roots are exposed.

Grouping plants

Certain plants will require different amounts of water throughout the year. Some spring-flowering bulbs go through a dormant stage during the summer and require little or no water at that time. Cucumber or melon plants, on the other hand, will be incredibly thirsty during the summer. Group plants with similar requirements together to help with your watering routine and to avoid accidentally watering plants that don't require it. This principle applies when damping down, too (see overleaf).

Water temperature

If possible, use water that is the same temperature as the growing environment. In early spring, I place a couple full watering cans under the bench in my greenhouse so that the temperature of the water is higher than it would be if taken straight from a faucet or a rain barrel outside. This avoids shocking young plants with cold water.

Hanging baskets and other container plants will need more water than plants in the ground, while seedlings benefit from sitting in a seed bath to soak up water from below.

Automatic systems

Automatic watering systems can be expensive to install, but if you are away from your greenhouse for a prolonged period, they can be invaluable. The most efficient type is a drip irrigation system, which pumps water through pipework to nozzles that are inserted into a root ball to gradually meet the plant's needs with no wastage. Solar-powered kits are available online and easy to set up (see below). These systems need monitoring to ensure the settings are correct for the plants' stage of growth, as plants are sensitive to overwatering when young or as temperatures fall.

The benefit is that you can choose a drip system that delivers precisely the amount of water you require at specific times of year. Crops such as tomatoes, for example, will benefit from consistent moisture levels during the summer to produce better-quality fruit.

The disadvantage of automatic systems is that they remove the gardener's instinct to react to the changing environment. On hot days, we can deliver more water and damp down as needed (see below) and reduce watering on colder days. In early and mid-spring, when we might have a warm, dry morning followed by a cold, wet afternoon, an automatic system cannot give a tailored response the way a gardener can.

Ultimately, automated irrigation systems suit some people more than others. Their level of sophistication is wide-ranging, as is the budget required to purchase them.

Damping down

Damping down simply means applying water to the greenhouse floor and underneath the staging to increase humidity within the space. Apart from a few exceptions, such as cacti and succulents, most greenhouse plants will require a degree of humidity during the summer to sustain healthy growth. It helps reduce the air temperature and the amount of transpiration (water loss) from your plants, aids pollination and fruit development, and encourages buds to open. Several pests, such as red spider

Set up a solar-powered irrigation system

With no need for access to utility water or electricity, a solar-powered system is simple and quick to set up.

01
Use an old bottle as a reservoir to hold the water. Add liquid fertilizer if you wish to feed plants, too. Place the solar panel in the ground in full sunlight.

02
Connect the pump, solar panel, and irrigation pipes to the control box.

03
Insert the drippers into each plant's root ball.

01

02

03

Damping down is essential for humidity-loving plants, but also to reduce extreme temperatures.

mites, can be kept under control by damping down, too, as high humidity levels are more uncomfortable for them, slowing their population growth.

The amount of damping down we carry out will depend on the outdoor conditions. At the height of summer, when the atmosphere in the greenhouse feels very dry, we should be damping down once or twice a day. The trick is to provide the right amount of humidity for the right plants. Zoning a greenhouse (see page 46) or grouping plants with similar needs will help get the best from them. Those plants that require lower humidity and greater air circulation are best situated near doors. Tomatoes generally prefer a drier atmosphere, but plants like eggplants, cucumbers, and melons are much happier in an environment with higher humidity levels. This group of plants is best situated away from the doors or large vents. In these higher-humidity areas, it is worth damping down a couple times a day during warm, sunny days. I will often damp down around that group of plants first thing in the morning and again in the early afternoon, encouraging a slightly drier environment going into the evening.

The water source you use for damping down does not matter; the water should not come into contact with the foliage, so rainwater, utility water, or even gray water such as bath water can be reused to create that humid atmosphere. Always try to avoid spraying the leaves of your plants with water during very hot periods, as this will scorch and damage them. By damping down, we should be creating the humidity we need without spraying the plants at all.

Composting

Every gardener who grows plants in a greenhouse of any shape or size will have a variety of options available to them when it comes to composting.

You may be in a position where you can compost outside of your greenhouse in an area at the bottom of the garden, or it may be that you only have enough room or only wish to process most of your green waste and/or kitchen waste within the greenhouse itself. There are a couple compact and effective ways to do this, giving us the added benefit of liquid fertilizer and, in some cases, heat as well as usable compost. Both methods outlined here will be an effective way of managing your kitchen waste within your greenhouse with small amounts of foliage from your greenhouse plants.

Wormery composting

Composting your kitchen waste and a little greenhouse waste in a wormery or worm bin will produce a soil improver you can use in your greenhouse, as well as a liquid fertilizer ("worm tea"). This method relies on a mixture of worm species consuming the waste and converting it into compost; these are not the same as earthworms. The specific species will eat a host of household waste, from fruit and vegetable peelings, cardboard and paper, and a small amount of bread and pasta. There are many benefits to using a wormery within your greenhouse. These include:

- Reducing your household waste through an organic recycling method.
- Accelerated composting, which also produces a highly nutritious liquid fertilizer.
- Compost from the wormery can be added to potting mix and can help increase beneficial microbes and soil structure.

Your wormery will often take several months to produce compost, and like many other composting systems, the variety of material is key. At least 25 percent of what you add to your wormery needs to be dry, brown material–such as cardboard and shredded paper–to keep the environment aerated. Grass clippings and excessive amounts of foliage should not be composted in a wormery, as the quick-release ammonia will have the potential to harm the worms. Waterlogging and oversaturation will also be harmful; a moist environment instead of a saturated one is preferable.

Advantages of putting your wormery in a greenhouse

- Effective composting all year round, as optimum worm activity is within a temperature range of 55–77°F (13–25°C).
- A regular supply of worm tea will help enhance soil fertility and stimulate plant growth. A dilution rate of 1:10 should be used for plants that have outgrown 3½in (9cm) pots. Avoid using the fertilizer on seedlings and cuttings.
- A wormery is an interesting and sustainable way of recycling within your greenhouse.

How to use a wormery

Set up the casing of your wormery according to the manufacturer's instructions, with a tap, reservoir, lid, and working trays. Take time to read up on the mechanics of how your wormery is put together and check that it is secure and sound before adding any worms or organic material. Purchase your composting worms from a specialist supplier. Above the reservoir, where any surplus water will gather, half fill your first organic matter layer with your presoaked bedding block (the compostlike material to start your worms off). When you add the worms, they will head down into the bedding to avoid the light. Keep the lid off your wormery to encourage them down.

01

01
Regularly add a layer of approximately 3¼in (8cm) of kitchen waste to the top tray of your wormery, including a small amount of garden waste and 25 percent brown material.

02

02
Leave to allow the worms to eat through the waste. If the waste is not being consumed, stop feeding for a few days.

03

03
Regularly drain the excess liquid from your wormery and dilute with water to 1:10 as a liquid feed for plants in a 3½in (9cm) pot or larger. After several months, finished compost will collect in the bottom tray, ready to be removed and used.

Add waste to your wormery a little at a time consistently to avoid overwhelming them while keeping the process moving at a steady rate.

Hot-bin composting

Hot-bin composting relies on oxygen, bacteria, and heat to accelerate the decomposition process of kitchen and greenhouse waste. Heat is a natural by-product of decomposition and is retained in the thickly insulated walls of the bin and then released slowly through a valve at the top. The heat and steam that is generated from this system has its benefits in the greenhouse during the winter, supplementing any heating to maintain the temperature above freezing.

This composting system has the potential to recycle a wider variety of waste than a wormery and to produce compost faster. It can process cooked food and perennial weeds due to the high temperature, with compost being produced in 30 to 90 days. A finer compost is produced the longer it is in the bin.

As with wormeries, a by-product of hot-bin composting is the ability to harvest liquid fertilizer, which can be diluted at a concentration of 1:10 and then used to promote strong, healthy growth in your mature greenhouse plants.

This type of composting does not require any turning, but the regular inclusion of wood chips, cardboard, and shredded paper will help aerate the material. As with wormeries, around 25 percent of woody or brown material, such as cardboard, should be added with any green waste.

Advantages of hot-bin composting

- Hot bins can process citrus, onions, and greater quantities of foliage and weeds.
- Due to high temperatures, perennial weeds in small quantities can be safely composted.
- The heat generated can supplement your greenhouse heating during winter.
- No turning is required due to the aerating effect of adding wood chips.
- Liquid fertilizer is produced to feed your greenhouse plants.
- Hot bins are discreet and streamlined.

A hot bin can process many kinds of waste and produces compost very quickly.

How to use a hot-bin composter

Set up your hot bin according to the manufacturer's instructions, ensuring that it locks together and is sound before adding any organic material.

01
Set up your base layer, which consists of easy-to-digest material, such as fruit and vegetable peelings and grass clippings, as well as wood chips and shredded paper for aeration.

02
Add a mixture of waste two or three times a week, gradually filling the bin. Do not layer your waste; mix it before it goes into the bin. The level will drop as the mixture breaks down, so keep feeding to maintain a high temperature.

03
At the same time, keep adding 25 percent of wood chips, cardboard, and shredded paper to keep the mixture aerated. Monitor the temperature inside the hot bin via the built-in thermometer. If the temperature drops, a bucketful of fresh grass clippings soon gets things going again.

04
Draw off surplus moisture from the tap regularly and use as a liquid feed, diluted 1:10 with water, on plants that are in a 3½in (9cm) pot or larger. Remove compost for use on your plants every 30–90 days.

01

02

03

04

Pollination

The majority of plants are either pollinated by the wind or by insects, and when growing in a greenhouse, there is the potential to exclude both. So, if we still expect our plants to produce fruit, it's up to us to give the pollination process a helping hand.

Some plants are grown for their seeds, such as nuts and wheat, but most of our greenhouse crops (tomatoes, citrus, and peppers, for example) are grown because they produce delicious fruit—the result of pollination. This is the vital process by which plants evolve their flowers into fruit for reproduction purposes. The fruit will accommodate the seeds within, providing the potential for the next generation of plants, and the setting of fruit will follow the exchange of pollen between flowers. Plants that produce swollen roots, such as carrots, or those that are cultivated for their leaves, like salads, do not require pollinating to produce the crop.

Aiding self-pollination

Flowers have male parts known as the stamen and female parts known as the stigma. Some plants will house both male and female parts within the same flower, while others, like cucumbers, will carry male and female parts on separate flowers.

Many greenhouse plants will be self-pollinating to a degree. Air movement inside the greenhouse will nudge some of the pollen grains from the stamen's anther to the stigma of the flower. To enhance pollination and maximize the potential yield, however, a little supplementary pollination is required. Self-pollination can be helped along by tapping or vibrating flowers to transfer pollen. This is the case for tomatoes, eggplants, and peppers. Cucumbers, melons, strawberries, apricots, and peaches will need additional help with pollination, either through insects or by hand. Strawberries and stone fruit, which produce flowers under glass in the late winter and early spring, cannot rely on natural insect pollination, as temperatures are often too cold for those insects to be active, so we must intervene to achieve a crop.

Pollinating by hand

To pollinate your greenhouse flowers by hand, you simply move pollen grains from the male part of the flower to the female part. This can be within the same flower or cross-pollinating neighboring flowers to achieve fertilization. When I hand-pollinate apricots and strawberries, I try to replicate the behavior of a pollinating insect using a small, soft paintbrush. Gently brush the male parts of the flower, then gently brush the female parts, depositing pollen as you go. Move that paintbrush around the flowers of the plant on several occasions over the course of a week or two to ensure maximum pollination.

Encourage pollination by drawing insects into the greenhouse or hand-pollinating with a small paintbrush.

Encouraging pollinators into the greenhouse

We can also aid pollination by enticing insects such as bees, moths, and butterflies into the greenhouse. Open vents and doors when outside conditions are favorable to give access to pollinators. The gentle air movement will increase pollination, as well as improving plant health by guarding against botrytis and rot. A plentiful supply of insect-friendly flowers in and around your greenhouse will also help attract more of these beneficial critters. Colonies of bumblebees are available to buy online to boost pollination in larger greenhouses or in gardens with low numbers of natural pollinators.

Providing hydration is also important. If you are harvesting rainwater in an open water tank, this will provide drinking water for pollinating insects. If not, a small saucer of water with some stones at the base (to prevent them from drowning while they drink) will help sustain insects, particularly during warm weather.

Pests and diseases

Certain pests and diseases are more prevalent under glass due to the protected environment, which favors their breeding cycle. When growing in a greenhouse, the adage that prevention is better than cure is very appropriate.

The growing conditions within a greenhouse encourage many pests and diseases. Temperatures are warmer and plant growth is enhanced, which goes hand in hand with a plentiful supply of soft, young shoots, which are particularly attractive to pests and vulnerable to disease. Good husbandry and diligent monitoring goes a long way to maintaining a healthy environment.

Natural remedies

Older techniques for pest and disease control under glass were reliant on creating a sterile environment, eradicating them from the greenhouse, but not discriminating against beneficial insects and pollinators. More modern techniques, especially those that utilize integrated management through biological controls, acknowledge that this isn't the healthiest solution.

As a result, chemical controls have fallen out of favor. After all, many of us use greenhouses to produce food and need to be discerning when it comes to the products we expose our plants to. Plus, we now have a greater understanding of the wider environmental harm caused by pesticides. Best practice is now to tackle the challenges of pests and diseases with natural remedies when possible.

Healthy defenses

Stressed plants that are regularly exposed to dry conditions or overcrowding and humidity will be more susceptible to pest and disease damage. Like us, if they are strong and buoyant, they will be far more resistant to diseases and pest attacks, so maintain the correct watering, good ventilation, and consistent feeding to keep your plants robust.

Small populations of pests in the greenhouse are tolerable if plant growth is not compromised, as low numbers will support a much wider ecosystem of predators, which we want to encourage. This is the basis on which biological controls are now used.

If any container plants become infested in the greenhouse, pest levels will often decrease when they are moved outside due to higher number of predators and less favorable breeding conditions.

Control options

If direct intervention is needed, it's best to physically remove pests by running your fingers along shoot tips or to use oil- or soap-based sprays (see opposite) to manage populations when you first see them. Alternatively, the idea of biological controls is to introduce natural predators to maintain a low level of pests instead of eradicating them completely. These can be sourced online, and your supplier will be able to advise on the minimum temperature at which your predator will be effective and at what time of year you should apply it.

Picking off the worst of the diseased foliage will help reduce the spread of infection. Good husbandry in the form of ventilation (see page 44), correct watering techniques (see page 112), and regular feeding will help plants resist infection and help us maintain a healthier greenhouse environment.

Tip

Place biological controls in your greenhouse at the end of the day, when it's cooler, and shut all doors and vents. The predators will emerge into your greenhouse and not be able to escape. Once they have found their food source, they will be more likely to inhabit your greenhouse longer term.

How to make a mildew preventative spray

1. Mix 1½oz (45g) of baking soda with 1 gallon (4.5 liters) of water.
2. Mix in 1 tbsp (15ml) of vegetable oil.
3. Add two drops of gentle dishwashing liquid.
4. Spray on the tops and bottoms of the leaves until the mixture drips off the foliage.

Best practice for pest and disease prevention includes (clockwise from top left) introducing natural predators such as ducks, which eat slugs; biological controls; oil- or soap-based sprays for aphids; and mildew spray.

Pests directory

The prevention of pests in a greenhouse through good husbandry is far more likely to keep numbers down than trying to control populations once they have a stronghold. Monitor your plants regularly and act quickly to get the best results.

Aphids

Small, sap-sucking insects ranging in color from green to black, brown, pink, or white. Colonies often form on the soft growth at the tips of stems, where the sap is more accessible.

Damage Aphids can spread viruses, as well as weakening the plant by continuous feeding. They digest large amounts of sap and secrete sticky honeydew, leading to sooty mold on the leaf surface, compromising photosynthesis and vigor.

Control measures Physically remove colonies as you see them, or regularly apply with oil- or soap-based sprays to limit spread. More severely affected plants can be relocated outside. Biological controls are also available but are only active during summer.

Mealybugs

Clusters of sap-feeding insects with a white, fuzzylike appearance when colonies form. This is created by their bodies being covered in a white wax powder.

Damage They often develop on leaves and stems, particularly on young growth and leaf joints. Persistent attacks will cause leaves to discolor, curl, and drop, and honeydew will lead to sooty mold.

Control measures Regular inspections and lightly brushing the bugs with denatured alcohol will help control levels. A high-pressure jet of water to physically remove the insects is another nonchemical solution.

Red spider mites

Resembling small spiders, these mites develop colonies around shoot tips, and when infestations grow, mottled or discolored leaves and distinctive webbing are present.

Damage As the foliage becomes discolored, photosynthesis is compromised and the plant eventually withers and dies. The mites mainly affect plants during the hottest summer months.

Control measures Increased humidity will deter population spread, and regular treatment with an oil- or soap-based spray will help control numbers. Severely infected plants should be removed from your greenhouse. Plants that are placed outside may recover, but if the attack is severe, you may need to compost the plant. For susceptible plants such as cucumbers, melons, and eggplants, keep humidity levels high during the summer as a preventative.

Aphids are sap-sucking and leave honeydew behind, leading to sooty mold.

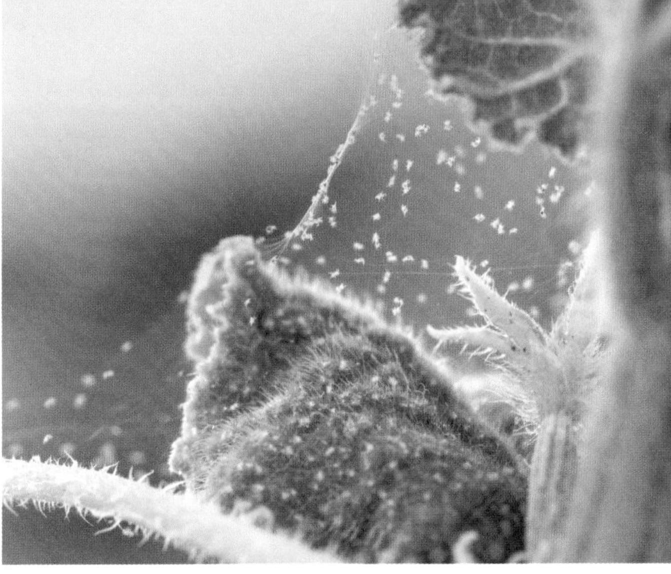

Mealybugs (above left) often cluster at leaf joints, while infestations of red spider mites (above) form distinctive webs.

Scale insects

Sap-feeding bugs characterized by their brown wax scales. They generally stay static on plants and feed relentlessly. Males can fly, but females often stay on the plant and create colonies.

Damage Leaves and young stems become infested, and as with many sap-feeding insects, they secrete honeydew, leading to sooty mold. Persistent infestations can weaken growth and make plants look unattractive. Fruits are rarely attacked, as this pest tends to target leaves and stems.

Control measures Lightly brush colonies with denatured alcohol to control numbers. Regular application and persistence is the only way to keep them under control. Scale insects can be particularly troublesome on citrus trees (see page 184).

Sciarid flies

Known as compost or mushroom flies, the larvae can be damaging to very young seedlings. Adults in small quantities are more of an irritation but can breed and create more larvae.

Damage The white larvae live in the soil and compost, where they feed on root hairs and the roots of seedlings, causing them to wither and die.

Control measures Sciarid flies are attracted to potting mix. Sticky yellow traps can help control adult populations, but maintaining a consistently moist but not waterlogged potting mix will help limit attacks, as larvae tend to thrive on plants that are under- or overwatered.

Slugs and snails

Soft-bodied mollusks that feed on plant growth.

Damage Irregular holes appear in most parts of the plant, including the fruits. Damage to young plants and seedlings can be detrimental and often occurs at night.

Control measures Regular cultivation and the disposal of eggs will help reduce populations. Beer traps and hollowed-out, upturned grapefruit skins draw in slugs and snails during the day and can be regularly disposed of. Alternatively, catch them on warm, humid evenings and either dispose of them or relocate them a good distance away to prevent their return.

Vine weevil

Attacks both garden and greenhouse plants. The white larvae are particularly damaging, as they attack plant roots, while the adults often leave characteristic notches in the edges of leaves. They are unable to fly but can crawl into greenhouses.

Damage The larvae feed on root tips and root systems, particularly of container-grown plants, which then checks the growth and causes shoots and leaves to wilt and collapse.

Control measures Regularly inspect plants for notches in the leaves and a loss of vigor. Keep your greenhouse clean and remove any dead and dying plant debris, as this is potential cover for adults to hide in. Avoid overwatering plants, as saturated potting mix allows the larvae to move freely within the root ball. Nematodes can be applied from spring until fall—this is particularly effective in container plants; it is best practice to apply these annually as a preventative.

Whitefly

Small, sap-feeding insects, often present on the underside of leaves. When an infested plant is disturbed, the winged insects emerge in a white cloud.

Damage Whiteflies secrete honeydew, leading to sooty mold, which leaves deposits on the upper surface of the leaf. This reduces photosynthesis and growth. Tomatoes and cucumbers are the most vulnerable greenhouse plants, but most others will be attractive to them.

Control measures Regular spraying with an oil- or soap-based spray at the first sign of attack will help keep populations low. Biological controls can also be introduced in the form of a parasitic wasp, but this requires warmer temperatures to be effective.

Woodlice

Hard-bodied crustaceans with up to seven pairs of legs. Often found in leaf litter and other decaying organic matter.

Damage Seedlings can be vulnerable and eaten off at soil level, with other parts of the plant attacked by a gnawing action. Most damage occurs at night, but woodlice can usually be found during the day hiding near damaged plants under pots, stones, or seed trays.

Control measures Keep the greenhouse clean. Avoid the accumulation of plant debris and piles of old pots to reduce the number of places for woodlice to hide and breed. They are attracted to foodstuffs such as cheese and sugar. A small amount placed near an upturned pot will be an attractive place to hide; they can then be relocated or disposed of.

Whiteflies gather on the underside of leaves and feed on the plant's sap.

Diseases directory

Good greenhouse hygiene and maintaining strong, healthy plants should help ward off most diseases, as will keeping control of pest populations.

Gray mold

Forms a gray, moldlike growth on stems, buds, and flowers, causing die-back and discoloration.
Damage The fungal growth leads to rotting tissue on leaves, stems, and buds.
Control measures Maintain good greenhouse hygiene, increase ventilation, and reduce overcrowding. Remove affected tissue at the first signs of damage to prevent spread.

Powdery mildew

Whitish mycelial growth coats the leaf surface as a parasite, spreading to shoots and buds with a characteristic powdery appearance.
Damage Discolored and distorted growth is followed by the slow decline of the plant, leading to death.
Control measures Increase ventilation and humidity levels. Physically remove the affected leaves and feed with a balanced fertilizer to encourage replacement growth and boost the plant's immunity. Treat with a preventive spray (see page 123).

Sooty mold

Black or brown sootlike deposits appear on the leaf surface due to the secretions of various sap-feeding insects.
Damage Although there is no direct damage caused by sooty mold, the compromised photosynthesis can take its toll.
Control measures Reduce sap-sucking pest populations and wash the fungus off the leaves to improve photosynthesis. Regular feeding will also help boost the plant's immunity and generate fresh foliage.

Diseases such as gray mold (top) and powdery mildew (right) can distort, discolor, and kill off plant growth.

What to grow

Edibles

The range of edible crops that can be grown in a greenhouse is vast, from fast-growing, exotic crops that revel in the higher temperatures of summer to the slower-growing crops that enjoy protection from the rain and cooler temperatures of the winter.

One of the main objectives when writing this book was to demonstrate how to grow as many crops as possible in a greenhouse. Making the decision to grow your own food goes far beyond any economic motive–in fact, there'll be no great financial saving. Instead, the intense taste compared to store-bought fruits and vegetables, as well as knowing exactly what's gone into producing your food and the environmental benefits of growing your own, are far more impactful. These are the real–and joyful–reasons to eat more seasonally from your greenhouse.

Choosing what to grow

Your greenhouse is your own, and you will have certain plants you want to grow and some you don't. If you have a particular liking for tomatoes, there's no reason why you can't indulge in a whole host of types, from cherry, to beefsteak, to tumbling and bush forms. While there are challenges to growing a wide range of plants that require different conditions, zoning your greenhouse will help create warmer and more humid environments in some parts, with drier and better ventilated sections in others (see page 46).

Easy-to-grow crops for beginners

- Herbs (see page 132)
- Salads (see page 136)
- Tomatoes (see page 140)
- Lemongrass (see page 168)
- Ginger (see page 172)
- Strawberries (see page 176)

Beefsteak tomato 'Costoluto Fiorentino', with its large, ribbed fruits, thrives grown under glass.

More advanced crops to try

- Eggplants (see page 146)
- Cucumbers (see page 156)
- Melons (see page 156)
- Chilies (see page 150)
- Sweet potatoes (see page 164)
- Peaches (see page 180)
- Apricots (see page 180)
- Citrus (see page 184)

If you are new to greenhouse gardening, I would advise you to start with a small group of edibles that you enjoy eating. Your instincts will then evolve, and you can feel your way through watering (see page 112) and ventilation (see page 44) to the point where you achieve success. Once you feel more confident in your growing ability and the way you use your space in the greenhouse, you can start to roll out some different crops and increase diversity as your comfort level and competency grows.

Year-round crops

With the range of edible plants that can be grown in a greenhouse, there is no reason why growing under glass should demand your attention only in the summer. Try to avoid falling into that trap where your greenhouse becomes a storage facility for barbecues and furniture in the winter, then, after a good clean-out in the spring, accommodates a few tomatoes or peppers.

The wide range of edibles, particularly those that are suited to your greenhouse during the winter and spring, should be all the encouragement you need to inhabit your greenhouse 12 months of the year. Placing your structure where it can be easily accessed allows you to be able to enjoy growing plants in it right the way through the year.

Try popular greenhouse edibles such as cucumber 'Telegraph Improved' (top) or strawberry 'Cambridge Favourite' (right).

Herbs

Mediterranean herbs relish a warm and free-draining spot to grow successfully, which is easily replicated in a greenhouse. The extra shelter and protection from the winter rain, along with the exaggerated temperatures in the summer, make our greenhouses the perfect place to grow Mediterranean herbs all year round.

There are many delicious options to choose from when deciding what herbs to grow under glass, no matter the time of year. During winter, when the greenhouse provides shelter and additional warmth to bring hardier herbs into leaf, we can achieve harvests of fresh parsley and mint earlier than if grown outside. In summer, when temperatures are higher in a greenhouse than in our gardens, crops like basil relish the heat and grow with more vigor, making the perfect accompaniment for tomatoes.

Parsley

Parsley can be grown from seed from January onward, using the protection offered by your greenhouse. To harvest parsley during the winter, to save time, and to achieve instant results, potted herbs from a supermarket can be planted in containers or raised beds to be harvested until late spring.

Simply remove the parsley plant from its container and plant into peat-free potting mix with 8in (20cm) between plants. Water thoroughly after planting, and do not allow the plants to dry out. As growth rates increase when temperatures rise, a weekly feed of a seaweed-based fertilizer will help promote fresh growth and prevent premature flowering. Hot and dry conditions will encourage your parsley to flower, so once flowering has taken place, compost the plant and replace with a greenhouse crop more suited to the warmer conditions of the summer. A parsley plant should grow happily and not need replacing if kept moist and cool until late April or May. During the summer, parsley is more suited to growing in containers outside or in the garden.

Supermarket parsley can be planted up in a raised bed for instant herbs that will last.

Mint

In the fall, when we would usually assume that the growing season for mint is coming to an end, it is possible to divide clumps and repot them.

Dividing mint

Placing divided new plants in an unheated greenhouse will provide us with a fresh crop of mint in the late winter and early spring.

Instructions

01
Either lift a small clump of mint from the garden or remove the root ball from a container.

02
Use a pair of pruners to cut viable, fist-sized clumps of mint away from the parent plant. The clumps will probably have signs of fresh shoots emerging from the soil, with fresh white roots just below the surface.

03
Any container that has drainage holes will be suitable for growing your mint; fill it to the top with peat-free potting mix. Depending on the size of your pot, either place a single clump of mint in the center or a group of two or three spaced out.

04
Firm each clump of mint into the surrounding soil by lightly pressing down with your fingers, creating a gap of 1in (2.5cm) between the top of the potting mix and the top of the pot to allow space for watering.

05
Position your pot of mint in a well-lit, unheated greenhouse and water well to settle the compost. Water frequently enough to keep the root ball from drying out, but do not overwater, as this may lead to rotting. You will be able to harvest fresh mint from late winter to late spring. Then the pot can be transferred to a place outside where it can continue to grow and be harvested for the summer. A weekly feed of a seaweed-based fertilizer will help promote healthy growth.

01

02

03

04

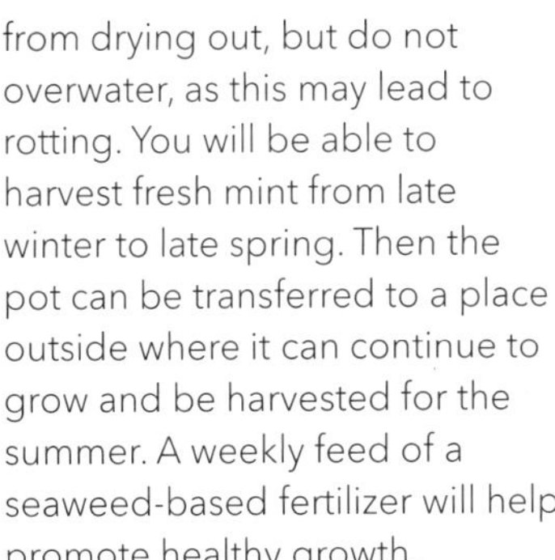

05

Cilantro

Cilantro is a wonderfully tasty herb to grow and enjoy in late spring and early summer. Seeds can be started off in your greenhouse in late winter and early spring by sowing two or three into cell trays of peat-free potting mix. Lightly cover with vermiculite or sieved compost and place in a frost-free greenhouse until germination has occurred. Cilantro can be successfully sown every four weeks for continued cropping.

Cilantro cell trays can be planted up in an unheated greenhouse for an earlier crop or out in the garden with a little protection initially from a cloche for a slightly more delayed crop. As soon as your cilantro has gone to seed or begins to flower, those stems can be used as cut flowers, but beyond that, those plants should be composted. Like parsley, cilantro plants are easy to get a hold of all year round. Those from a supermarket comprise of lots of seedlings that can be divided into clumps and grown on (see page 107). Like many leafy herbs, a greater growing space with less competition will encourage more leafy growth and deter flowering.

Sow cilantro seeds two or three to a cell tray every four weeks for a regular crop.

Basil

There are many ways to grow basil for our greenhouses and summer containers. Sow a pinch of seeds into a cell tray of peat-free potting mix and lightly cover with vermiculite or sieved compost in late spring. That pinch of seed should create a small clump of basil seedlings, which can then be potted on or planted into hanging baskets or containers in the greenhouse when temperatures increase in midsummer, or they can happily be grown outside.

A basket of basil will thrive in the summer greenhouse.

Supermarket basil can be planted directly into raised beds or containers in your greenhouse, but this herb dislikes cooler temperatures, so waiting until late April before potting on would be advisable. Alternatively, it is easy to root cuttings of supermarket basil in water (see opposite).

Basil cuttings

This handy technique can transform a cheap supermarket plant into numerous healthy plants.

Instructions

01
Remove a 4in (10cm) basil shoot, cutting just below a leaf joint.

02
Remove the leaves from the lower half of the cutting with scissors to avoid foliage being submerged in the water, which will lead to rot and deterioration.

03
Place the basil cutting in a glass of water so that the remaining foliage is above the surface of the water. Put on a sunny windowsill but out of the direct heat of the midday sun. Replace the water every few days to prevent bacteria from building up.

04
When fresh roots have emerged at the base of the cuttings, transfer into 3½in (9cm) pots of peat-free soil and water well.

05
The transition from growing in water to growing in potting mix can be challenging for your cuttings for the first few days. Sit your freshly potted-up cuttings in a tray of water so the potting mix remains saturated, allowing them to adjust to the new rooting environment. After a few days, remove the container from the tray of water to acclimatize to the greenhouse or windowsill environment. The mother plant can be potted up to allow it to grow on and provide a fresh crop of basil leaves for more cuttings or for use in the kitchen.

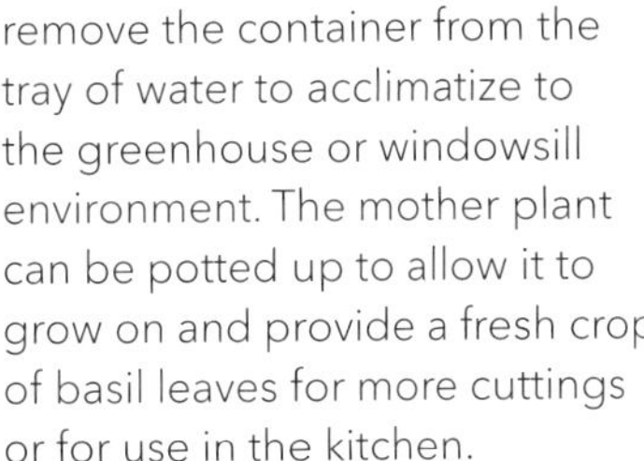

01

02

03

04

05

Salad leaves

Bagged salad must be one of the most popular things to throw into our shopping carts at the grocery store, yet salad crops are some of the easiest vegetables to grow at home, regardless of the size of your greenhouse.

Growing hardy salads is the perfect way to produce food from your greenhouse, at a time of year when few other plants will tolerate those cooler conditions and reduced light levels.

High summer temperatures in your greenhouse will make growing leafy salads more challenging, with poor germination rates and plants tending to become stressed and produce flowers. So during summer, salad crops are best grown in containers and beds outside. It is when the light levels drop and the cooler temperatures arrive that the greenhouse becomes a perfect place to grow salad.

Cut-and-come-again salad leaves are easy to grow, and by regularly removing the outer leaves, you can have a fresh supply for months.

Growing salads under cover

Suitable for sowing into cell trays or directly into open ground, raised beds, and containers, versatile winter salad leaves—such as mustards, winter lettuce, and hardy spinach—will work hard for you, and the seeds are easy to germinate in a greenhouse when conditions are less favorable in the garden.

Once you have cleared out the summer crops, sow various salad leaves in cell trays and grow on until the seedlings are ready to plant up into pots or directly into the ground or raised beds in your greenhouse to continue growing under cover. Most general-purpose, peat-free potting mixes are suitable for growing salad leaves.

Plants grow slowly during winter, when light levels and temperatures are low, so you'll likely be harvesting from a September-sown crop until early spring, when a February-sown crop will be ready to replace them. Winter lettuce, for example, will often be ready for harvesting as a head in February/March if sown in September under glass. I'd recommend 'Winter Density', 'All Year Round', and 'Arctic King' for growing in your greenhouse.

From late spring into summer, when growth is more rapid, continue to sow in small batches every few weeks. If your tomatoes, eggplants, and cucumbers start to slow their production toward the end of summer, make sure you have a few trays of salad ready to go.

Salads sown in fall in an unheated greenhouse will last until early spring.

Instructions

01
Fill a cell tray with peat-free potting mix to the top and water well to settle the mix, which allows ½in (1cm) or so for sowing seeds and covering with either potting mix or vermiculite.

02
Sow two or three seeds per cell tray on the moist surface of the potting mix.

03
Cover with a light dusting of potting mix using a sieve. Water from underneath when dry, and when seedlings emerge, thin out by trimming with a pair of scissors to leave the strongest seedling.

04
When seedlings are large enough to handle and roots are appearing through the drainage holes of the cell, plant out 8in (20cm) apart in an unheated greenhouse or in a greenhouse that is heated to prevent frost in fertile, weed-free soil. To increase soil fertility, add a 2in (5cm) layer of well-rotted garden potting mix to the surface and lightly fork in prior to planting.

05
Water in well. Keep the soil moist but not overly wet during the winter, as this will lead to rot and disease.

01

02

03

04

05

Once seeds have germinated and produced a second pair of leaves, apply a seaweed feed once a week to keep the plants in top condition.

Winter salads

These salad crops can all be sown in the fall and grown through winter into spring in a cool, unheated greenhouse with diminished light levels:

- Kale (grown as a baby leaf)
- Parsley
- Pea shoots
- Chervil
- Chives
- Chop suey greens
- Corn salad
- Mustards
- Mibuna
- Mizuna
- Arugula
- Beets
- Landcress
- Pak choi
- Lettuce (winter types, such as butterheads and cos)

Growing seedlings to plant out

Salad crops are very sensitive to weather conditions; exposure to light, warmth, and water will greatly increase their growth rate. So when the weather warms up, I like to sow a fresh batch of spring and summer salads every four weeks once I've planted out a set of young plants, making an eight-week cycle from sowing to replacing.

These salads can be grown from seed in the greenhouse, and when the young plants are established enough, they can be acclimatized in a cold frame before being planted up outside to grow unchecked and successfully under the added protection of a cloche. Cloche-grown salads will crop several weeks earlier than those grown in the open ground, and that extra protection enables us to grow more sensitive crops that would otherwise fail.

Instructions

01

Once your spring salad seedlings are strong enough to plant out, harden them off in a cold frame first for a week or so to acclimatize them to the cooler conditions outside.

02

Using a string line as a guide, plant the seedlings in rows spaced 10in (25cm) apart in a raised bed.

03

Water well and cover with a tunnel cloche (see page 32). Lift the cloche to water plants as needed. Do not let the soil dry out; maintain a reasonable level of moisture to encourage growth but not too much to cause rot and disease.

01

02

03

Harvesting

Most salad plants grow from a central point, where leaves develop and fresh foliage emerges from the middle of the plant. To prolong and increase your crop, simply pick the outer, more developed leaves, which will in turn be replaced from the productive center. Avoid removing that central growing core for a continuous supply of leaves.

Regularly picking the outer leaves of lettuce plants will give a far larger quantity of salad than waiting to cut a full head of lettuce. However, if you prefer harvesting as an entire plant, resow and replant lettuces every four weeks in summer.

Soaking leaves in water for 20 minutes before you eat them will not only hydrate them, but also make any pests float to the surface (including tiny slugs and snails), where they can be easily removed.

Pests

Greenhouse pests are at lower levels during the winter, but stay vigilant and monitor for aphids. Like other sap-sucking pests, aphids will congregate on young growth. Simply remove the aphids with your fingers or apply an organic oil or soap-based spray on a weekly basis until populations are reduced.

Slugs and snails may wish to share your salad; these can be easily picked off by hand. Beer traps or upturned grapefruit-skin traps are also useful to help keep slug and snail numbers at bay.

If your salad leaves start to produce flowers, simply remove them. If their vigor continues to be compromised, clear the plants and replace them.

Winter salad leaves can be picked through the colder months before replacing with a spring crop.

Tomatoes

A homegrown tomato warmed by the sun is one of the greatest pleasures for a greenhouse gardener. It will deliver a flavor unrivaled by any store-bought fruit.

Cordon beefsteak tomatoes will be at home even in a small lean-to greenhouse.

When we think about food that we can grow in our greenhouses, one of the first plants that springs to mind is the tomato. Growing under glass offers this member of the potato family a little extra warmth in the early spring and late summer, creating a longer growing season for us to take full advantage of.

Propagation

Tomatoes are easily grown from seed but need a heated propagator or sunny windowsill to germinate, even if your greenhouse is heated to a frost-free setting, as a temperature of around 68°F (20°C) is needed to trigger growth.

Seeds should be sown thinly into 3½in (9cm) pots of peat-free potting mix and lightly covered with vermiculite or sieved compost in early March. Once consistent germination has occurred, the extra humidity within the heated propagator may cause the seedlings to damp off (see page 97), so remove the lid at this point to acclimatize them. Prick out into individual 3½in (9cm) pots to grow on.

Planting

The most popular ways to grow tomatoes in greenhouses are in raised beds, large pots, or grow bags. Remember, they will grow big over the course of the summer, and although it's tempting to cram plants together, this will compromise their vigor.

Planting into raised beds or borders will allow the greatest root run and means plants will dry out less frequently. Adding well-rotted garden compost every spring before planting will help increase biological activity and fertility within the soil.

Sow tomato seeds in early March, then prick out (far left) into individual pots for growing on through summer.

Trailing tomatoes (left) will grow happily in a hanging basket.

Planting can be repeated each year, but if a loss of vigor or disease affects the crop, a soil change or growing something different in that space for a couple years may be necessary. Using bags or containers for tomatoes during that time will be your best option.

A single beefsteak or cherry tomato grown as a cordon in a large container works well, as they have no competition for water and nutrients. With very large containers, you only need to replace the top 50 percent of medium with fresh peat-free growing medium each year. A hanging basket of tumbling tomatoes can utilize the roof space of your greenhouse, though be extra vigilant about watering to prevent them from drying out; most baskets will need watering daily. Bush tomatoes are well suited to large containers. Just avoid wetting the foliage, as this can lead to botrytis and blight.

Grow bags are also ideal for growing a crop of tomatoes. A standard grow bag can accommodate two tomato plants. Three is possible, although they will need more water and nutrition. Three cordon beefsteak tomatoes can even be accommodated in a small lean-to greenhouse in a grow bag, if the shelving is removed.

A well-rooted tomato plant will transition happily into any of these locations. I find that by sowing my tomatoes in March, they are ready to plant out in the first half of May, when temperatures are more stable and the risk of frost is reduced.

Caring for the crop

Whether you're growing cordon, bush, or trailing varieties, tomatoes thrive in a well-ventilated, warm, relatively dry environment.

Feeding

Once your individual plants begin to establish, start a weekly feed of seaweed fertilizer to help develop a strong root system and continue for the following six weeks, until mid-June, by which time they should be established in their final position.

By then, a healthy, well-fed tomato plant should have a strong structure with flowers starting to appear. At this point, switch to a potash-based fertilizer, which will support foliar and root development but will focus more on flowers and fruit production. Feed once a week until the end of the plant's productive life, often at the first frosts.

Training

Bush tomatoes by their very nature require little training. Growing tomatoes via the cordon method, however—where we remove all the side shoots to create a single supported stem to carry the fruit—ensures the greatest productivity from the smallest space. Whether you're training standard globe, beefsteak, or cherry types, string supports are the ideal option; bamboo canes also work well.

For cordons with larger fruits, the support needs to be approximately 6½ft (2m) in height to support five or six trusses. Supports for cherry types need to be around 10ft (3m) in height.

Instructions

01
Tie string to the roof space via the frame or horizontal wires.

02
Allow 12in (30cm) of surplus string to gather at the base of the planting hole.

03
Position your tomato plant in the hole on top of the coiled surplus string and a little deeper than the original soil level for extra stability. Fill in with compost.

04
Firm in well and water. Twist the developing stem around the string as it grows.

Tipping out

Due to their relatively short growing season (March to October), more than six trusses are unlikely to develop and will compromise any trusses lower down the plant. When your tomato plant has reached this point, remove the top to a leaf node above the final truss to concentrate the plant's energy on fruit that has already set. This will give you the best chance of ripened fruit before light levels and temperatures drop in fall.

There is no need to tip out the cherry types; allow these to grow until the end of the summer, although you may need to stop your cherry tomato plant by tipping out if it reaches the end of your support. My cherry tomatoes, for example, tend to go not only up the side of the greenhouse, but into the roof space, too. Any flowers produced in the fall can be removed, as they are unlikely to produce fruit and will hinder the ripening of developing ones.

Removing side shoots

To help develop a single stem for cordon types, remove side shoots. The shoots will appear at most leaf axils and should be pinched out as soon as they're large enough to handle. Small shoots can be pinched out by hand, while large shoots are best removed with scissors or pruners to reduce the risk of damaging the main stem. There is no need to remove side shoots from bush tomatoes or trailing types.

Pollination

Tomato plants are self-fertilizing. When the flower opens, pollen from the male parts of the flower (anthers) will fall onto the female parts (stigma). If your tomatoes are not setting, however, increase humidity, which will help pollen stick to the female parts of the flower—although in very wet conditions, pollen can sometimes not be released from the anthers. Extreme heat and cold may even cause pollen to be killed off. On warmer days, increased ventilation will help pollinators access your greenhouse and assist the process.

Pests and diseases

One of the main diseases that affects tomatoes is late blight, the risk of which is increased by cold, wet foliage at night. Water the soil around the plant, instead of the foliage, before 3 P.M. so your plants go into the evening with dry foliage.

Blossom end rot also affects tomatoes and is linked to a lack of calcium and irregular watering. At the height of summer, I water my tomatoes once in the morning and again in the early afternoon. This avoids exposing the root balls to very dry conditions, providing more stable moisture levels. Remove any affected fruits, and this husbandry should address any deformity.

Look out for whitefly and aphids and treat any early signs with a weekly spray of insecticidal soap or soap- or oil-based spray until populations are under control. Yellow sticky traps will help you monitor pest levels, and biological controls are also available.

Slugs and snails can be a threat, too. Upturned grapefruit skins and beer traps will help minimize populations, particularly in early stages of growth.

Yellow flowers should start to appear 5-7 weeks after planting out tomatoes.

Harvesting

As temperatures increase, you'll notice that your tomatoes ripen at a much faster rate; around 77°F (25°C) is ideal for most varieties. Harvest as soon as they have turned red so the plant's energy can then focus on the developing fruit. Remove lower leaves and congested areas of foliage to allow light and air to circulate around the fruit. This accelerates the ripening process, particularly at the end of summer.

Cherry types can be picked individually or by removing the entire truss with a pair of pruners or scissors. Gently cup larger fruits and lift, with the aim of detaching the fruit where the stem and the calyx (the green leaflike sepals at the top of the tomato) meet, so you can store the fruit without wounding it.

At the end of the growing season, remove any unripe fruits and bring them into your kitchen to ripen: Hang up trusses or place larger fruits in a bowl or brown paper bag with a ripening banana—this will emit ethylene, encouraging those last few stubborn tomatoes to ripen.

Beefsteak varieties such as 'Orange Wellington' and 'Costoluto Fiorentino' can be gently lifted from the plant.

Cherry tomatoes can be picked individually (above, far left) or removed in trusses (above, left).

Thinning out lower leaves (above) increases air circulation and light to aid the ripening process.

Calendar

January	-
February	-
March	Sow seeds
April	Prick out and pot on Feed with weekly seaweed fertilizer until mid-June
May	Plant out
June	Tie in Switch to potash-based fertilizer once a week
July	Harvest
August	Harvest
September	Harvest
October	Harvest and help develop unripened fruit
November	-
December	-

Recommended cultivars

- **'Baby Boomer'** A high-yielding bush type, which reaches approximately 18in (45cm) in height with red fruits.
- **'Black Cherry'** Something a little different; a cordon cherry with purple-skinned fruit and a rich flavor. It ripens early, too.
- **'Buffalosun'** Red-blushed yellow beefsteak tomato with resistance to late blight. Great flavor and a reliable cropper.
- **'Moneymaker'** A popular and easy-to-grow standard tomato with plenty of medium-sized, tasty red fruits.
- **'Sungold'** This firm favorite offers particularly sweet cherry tomatoes and abundant cropping with orange fruits.
- **'Supersteak'** Beefsteak with large red fruits, superb flavor and texture, plus good disease resistance.
- **'Tumbler'** One of the most popular for containers and hanging baskets; a dwarf tomato with a trailing habit, producing juicy, cherry-sized tomatoes.

'Tumbler' is a firm favorite with its cherrylike fruits and trailing habit.

Eggplants

Eggplants adore the warmth and will thrive in both containers and the ground, so growing them in our greenhouses during the summer is the perfect place to give them everything they need.

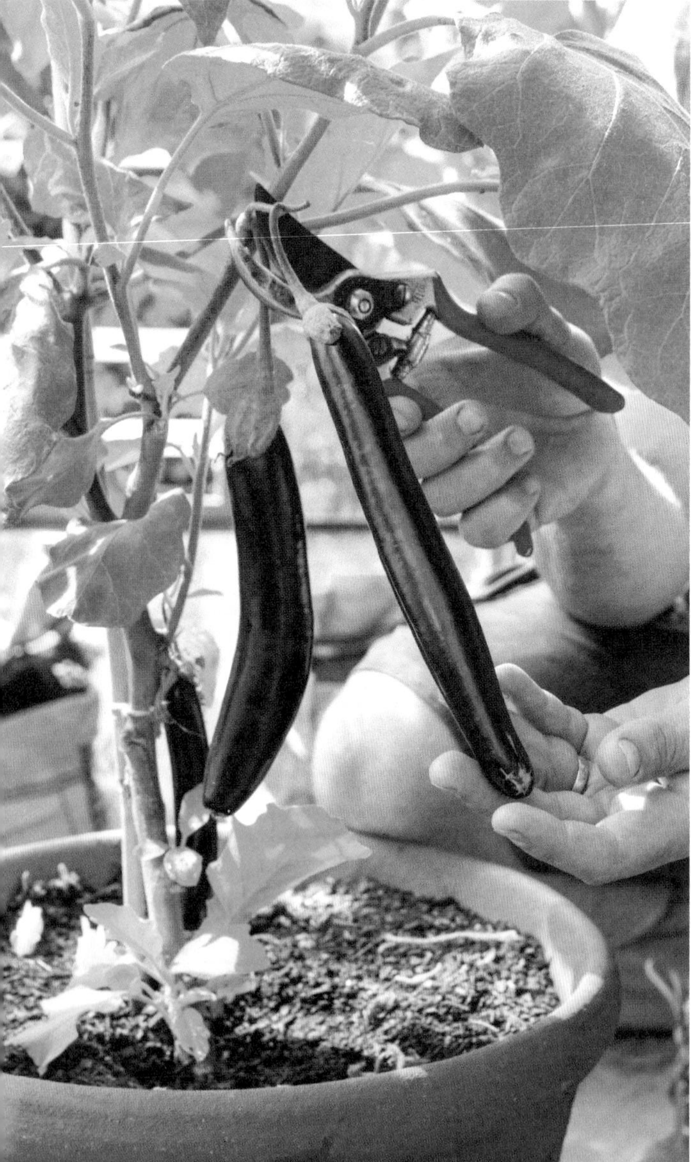

There is a huge choice of eggplants available to grow: from large, glossy, dark-purple fruits to egglike white eggplants and striped, long, thin sausagelike fruits. Adaptable to most containers, borders, or grow bags, and delicious roasted or grilled, this member of the tomato and potato family has a versatility that makes it a very welcome addition to the greenhouse in the summer.

Propagation

Also known as aubergines, eggplants can be grouped with chilies and tomatoes when it comes to sowing seed, as each plant in this trio requires warmth to germinate. A heated propagator is a good environment to raise young seedlings, with an ambient temperature of around 68°F (20°C). You'll probably only need three to five eggplant plants for a plentiful harvest, but it's a good idea to sow around twice as many seeds as you need in a 3½in (9cm) pot of peat-free potting mix to ensure you have enough. You can then prick out the strongest few seedlings to pot on.

An unusual eggplant, 'Farmers Long' is a prolific variety, with distinctive slender fruits.

Instructions

01
Sow your seeds on a prepared surface of well-watered potting mix, spacing them out using a wooden skewer if necessary.

02
Lightly cover with sifted compost or vermiculite so that you can no longer see the seed. Place in a heated propagator and wait for even germination before you remove the lid to acclimatize the seedlings to cooler temperatures. Keep them on the heated base for another week or two.

03
Keep your eggplants growing at a steady rate by pricking out the strongest seedlings into cell trays or directly into individual 2¾in (7cm) pots once the second "true" set of leaves appear. Water the medium in the new pot, then use a wooden skewer to lift each seedling gently, holding them by the first leaves. Transfer to the new pot and firm in gently.

01

02

03

Planting

Plants can be potted on into 3½in (9cm) pots when roots appear through the drainage holes at the base of the smaller pot. A well-rooted 3½in (9cm) pot will be the minimum size to plant an eggplant out into its final position, around the middle of May, when temperatures—particularly at night—are a little warmer. Eggplants are suitable for raised beds, large containers with a diameter of around 16in (40cm), or grow bags in the greenhouse (two plants per grow bag would be advisable). Any peat-free potting mix will work well with a supplementary feeding routine (see overleaf) to ensure the plants grow steadily and strongly, building a robust framework to carry the fruits later in the summer.

Caring for the crop

Eggplants will need the protection of a greenhouse until the end of June. During the summer, the plants can be put outside, which reduces pest levels. Those that are kept under glass, however, will grow larger and will not be slowed by the cooler evenings as fall approaches.

Eggplant flowers are self-pollinating; tie in flowering plants to a single cane support.

Feeding

These plants grow quickly in the warmth of the greenhouse during the early summer, so we need to fertilize the young plants to give them everything they need during this period. When young plants have been potted on from a cell tray into a small pot, a weekly seaweed-based fertilizer will help them establish strong roots and healthy growth. Continue with this weekly seaweed feed until the plants develop flowers and have achieved a strong framework robust enough to carry several large fruits. At the point where you have a good framework and those flowers begin to appear, switch to a weekly potash-based fertilizer, which can often be purchased in the form of a general tomato feed. The increase in potash will help promote flowering and fruit development. Continue with the weekly potash feed until the frosts or all fruit has been harvested.

Training

Most eggplant plants will require a single bamboo cane for support. Loosely tie your eggplant to the cane as it grows. I find that most eggplants branch naturally, but some cultivars may end up with a dominant shoot that needs tipping by removing the growing tip and the top two leaves if it reaches a height of around 20in (50cm).

Calendar

January	-
February	-
March	Sow seeds
April	Prick out and pot on
May	Plant out
June	Stake plants
July	Harvest
August	Harvest
September	Harvest
October	-
November	-
December	-

The key to reasonable-sized fruit is restricting the number of eggplants on your plant to around five or six, which are well spaced throughout. Remove any crowded fruits to allow those five or six to develop with plenty of space and air around them.

Pests and diseases

Eggplants can be one of the first plants in the greenhouse to attract whitefly, aphids, and red spider mites. Monitor for any aphids or whitefly and either physically remove them or spray with insecticidal soap or an oil- or soap-based spray until populations are under control. Red spider mites can be deterred with higher levels of humidity, so planting your eggplants in a more humid environment with your cucumbers and melons helps reduce the risk of an infestation. Extreme infestations of red spider mites and whitefly can be reduced by placing your eggplants outside during July and August, as the outdoor conditions tend to be less favorable to these pests, and populations are often reduced.

Alternatively, preempt whitefly and red spider mites by ordering biological controls when your plants are young and introduce predators, periodically during the summer. A small coir mat makes a perfect launch site for your predators, which can be positioned within the canopy of the eggplant or next to young plants that do not have a branch structure yet.

Harvesting

Eggplants can be removed from the parent plant when they have fully ripened, which can be determined by a little give in the flesh when you squeeze gently between your fingertips and by strong coloration of the fruit. Use a pair of pruners to cut the eggplant away with a short section of stalk at the top to help with storage and prevent the top of the fruit from becoming damaged or rotten.

Recommended cultivars

- **'Black Beauty'** An incredibly popular and reliable eggplant with dark, glossy purple fruits. Easy to grow and widely available.
- **'Farmers Long'** A tall variety that produces slender, long purple eggplants that can reach around 12in (30cm) in length. Great fun to grow for something a little different, and useful in the kitchen due to the small slices that can be achieved.
- **'Meatball'** A whopping cultivar that is a lot of fun to grow, with a sweet, dense flavor and fruits that can achieve over 5in (12cm) across.
- **'Pinstripe'** A more compact type that is suitable for containers or smaller spaces, such as balconies or smaller greenhouses. Purple fruits with distinctive white stripes make this a little more unusual than most.

Eggplants such as 'Meatball' should be thinned to five or six fruits to allow full development.

Chilies and peppers

Chilies and peppers originate from Mexico and absolutely adore the heat that a greenhouse can provide during the summer. Plus, their fruiting season can be extended as fall approaches due to the warm environment within the greenhouse, and with regular picking and overwintering, successional fruiting can be achieved.

Regular cropping of chilies and peppers gives remaining fruits the space to develop.

It is one of the great benefits of growing capsicums—a group of plants that covers a wide variety of chilies and bell peppers—in a greenhouse that they relish the high temperatures in the summer. It is the colder months, when light levels are lower, that are the most problematic for these plants, as they are very quick to tell you that they're not happy—especially if they're too cold or wet or sitting in a draft. Any temperature below 54°F (12°C) will likely kill them.

Capsicums are a mixed bag regarding the heat that they give. Chilies can vary tremendously, and their heat is measured by the Scoville scale (see box below). Be sure to research the varieties of chilies that you grow to understand the heat that the fruits will offer. I've been caught out in the past when making batches of chili oil—some offered a very warm and mild flavor, while others have nearly made steam come out of my ears. Not all chilies are culinary, either; many have been bred for decorative purposes and offer interest toward the end of the summer and fall in ornamental containers.

The Scoville scale

In 1912, American chemist Wilbur Scoville developed a way to measure the heat of chilies by concentrating the fruit into a solution and diluting it with sugar syrup until the heat could no longer be detected by a panel of tasters. The more the chili had to be diluted, the greater the heat and the higher the Scoville rating. If a chili was diluted 100,000 times, it would register 100,000 Scoville Heat Units on the scale. A scorching bhut jolokia chili, for example, registers 1,000,000 on the scale, while a mild jalapeño registers 2,500–8,000.

When staking chili and pepper plants, place a small pot on top of each cane to protect your eyes.

Preserve chilies by hanging bunches in your greenhouse to dry, for a culinary and decorative winter treat.

Overwintering chilies

Chilies will not tolerate a frost and dislike cold temperatures, so the best way to overwinter them is by bringing your chili plant indoors (if practical and your plant isn't enormous). The likelihood is that your chili plant will drop its leaves due to the low light levels, so watering should be minimal during this time–just enough to keep the plant alive. Place your chili in the sunniest part of your home and increase watering when growth begins in the spring. It's best to repot your chili at this time, too.

Did you know?

Chilies can be dried in the roof space of your greenhouse. Cut the fruit with a length of stem attached and bunch them together using an elastic band, which will retract as the stems dry. The chilies are usually dry within a few weeks and can be stored decoratively, hung up in the kitchen, for use in the winter.

Propagation

Although there are many chili and pepper plants that we can buy from garden centers and nurseries in the spring, there is a far greater diversity available through growing them from seed. Chili and pepper seeds need warmth to trigger germination, and this is best achieved using a heated propagator. Once reasonable germination has occurred, the seedlings can be hardened off (see page 25) by removing the lid from the propagator, then, when large enough to handle, prick them out into single pots or modules. We need to encourage young chilies and peppers to grow quickly and establish a strong framework before they begin to produce flowers later in the year. This is achieved by regularly potting on the plants to ensure that growth does not become checked or stunted by root restriction.

Planting

Chilies and peppers can be grown successfully in raised beds, open ground, or containers. Pots work well, as you can supplement their nutrition with liquid feed to achieve a strong framework early on and then add potash to help the flowering and fruit development. Plants that can achieve a greater height will grow well in a large pot due to their rate of growth, while dwarf chilies and decorative types are much better suited to smaller containers. However, chilies and peppers are equally at home in borders or raised beds in a greenhouse. The process of growing and staking is the same, but when planting out, create a small depression around the plant to help capture water as the young plant establishes. They will generally need watering less frequently than those in pots and grow bags.

Instructions

01
Sow the seed on the surface of moist peat-free potting mix. Remember not to oversow, as this will lead to congested seedlings and wasted seed.

02
Label, then lightly cover the seed with vermiculite. Place in a heated propagator or on a sunny windowsill to encourage the seeds to germinate.

03
When the seedlings have two or three pairs of leaves, use a kebab stick to gently remove each one from the pot, handling the seedling by the first set of leaves. Avoid touching the stem, as you may damage the young plant.

01

02

03

04

05

04
Create a hole in the center of a 2¾in (7cm) pot of moist peat-free potting mix. Gently guide the fragile roots of one seedling into the potting mix to a slightly greater depth than previously grown.

05
Pot on when roots appear through the drainage holes at the base, then plant out into its final position, around mid-May.

06
Stake the growing plant with a single bamboo cane. Tie the plant to it as it grows.

07
Water into a shallow trench around the plant so it pools and directly accesses the roots.

06

07

Caring for the crop

Most capsicums require the same growing conditions and routines.

Feeding

Once you have pricked out your seedlings, start a feeding routine of a seaweed liquid fertilizer once a week. As the plant grows, transition to a higher-nitrogen feed, such as nettle fertilizer (see page 82). If foliage begins to turn lime green or yellow, that can be a reaction to the cold or a lack of nitrogen. If plants are warm and out of a draft, a lack of nutrition is most likely, so feed your plants twice a week with a nitrogen-rich fertilizer.

Plants should start to produce flowers in early summer. Those flowers can be encouraged with a high-potash fertilizer once a week to replace the nitrogen feed. Pollination will occur quite naturally, and increased humidity will help promote fruit setting while reducing red spider mite infestations. Increase humidity by damping down your greenhouse on warm, sunny days (see page 114).

Training

Most peppers and larger chilies will require some staking. Push a single bamboo cane into the potting mix at the center-back of the plant and gently tie the main stem to that cane as it grows. Remove the very tip of the young plant when it reaches 12in (30cm) to avoid a tall and leggy specimen. If young plants branch naturally and do not have a dominant stem, I tend not to remove their tips and allow the plant to develop its natural form. Some peppers can be heavy and cause some branches to snap, so monitor those branches and add extra support with string to the main cane to help lighten the load.

Very importantly, bell peppers should only produce around six to eight viable fruits distributed throughout the plant. As the fruits develop, remove young fruits that are crowded, aiming for each of the retained fruits to have sufficient space to grow. Regular cropping will help develop maturing fruits, but be conscious of the slowing rate of growth and ripening toward the end of the summer, which is why the number of fruits should be restricted.

Cut back the growing tip (left) to keep plants compact and bushy.

Thinning peppers (below) to six or so fruits will result in larger mature fruits.

Calendar

January	-
February	Sow seeds in a heated propagator
March	Prick out and pot on to keep the plants actively growing
April	Pot on young chili plants
May	Plant into final containers/beds
June	-
July	Harvest
August	Harvest
September	Harvest
October	Bring indoors to overwinter
November	-
December	-

Pests and diseases

A weekly spray of an oil- or soap-based organic product around the top third of the plant will help keep sap-sucking pests under control. Capsicum plants are particularly vulnerable in the early stages of growth, as any aphid attack will cause distortion and compromise the growth rate and, in turn, productivity later in the summer. Check plants regularly, and if infestations become too big, remove the pests with your fingers or a sponge.

Harvesting

Many capsicums will go through different colors as they ripen. Most chilies and peppers transition from green to a dark brown and then red, and the sweetness and heat of the fruit will increase with the ripeness. Underripe chilies and peppers are edible but sometimes bitter, so taste first if in doubt. Harvest ripened fruits to encourage flowers and more fruit later in the season.

Harvest ripened fruits from these heat-loving plants for a colorful array in summer.

Recommended cultivars

Chilies

'Cherry Bomb' An unusual-shaped chili with round, tomatolike fruits. Another easy-to-grow cultivar, which can reach a height of around 2ft (60cm) with generous cropping, with fruits that ripen to a bright-red color.

'Hungarian Hot Wax' Versatile in cooking and easy to grow. Vigorous growth with long, pointed fruits that can reach 4in (10cm) in length. Maturing from pale green to red when ripe, the heat increasing with age.

'Joe's Long' My 'go-to' for a traditional-looking chili. A vigorous form, which will reach around 2ft (60cm) in height and will produce green, slender fruits, which ripen to red. A perfect chili for drying.

Sweet peppers

'Diablo' A well-deserved award winner, which prolifically produces 6in (15cm) red fruits that are sweet and crisp. Will require staking and picking regularly to prevent the plant from becoming overloaded and snapping.

'Mohawk' An easy-to-grow, small fruiting type, which matures to a yellow/orange color when ripe. Not as tall as other peppers but will still require support. Perfect for container growing; remember to keep picking and feeding for a continuous supply of fruit.

'Red Star' A traditional bell type with bright-red fruits that are produced early compared to other bell peppers and easy to grow. Fruit can be harvested when green, but sweetness is increased as the fruits ripen.

Cucumbers and melons

Cucumbers and melons are both members of the cucurbit family and are not tolerant of frosts. These annual plants require the heat of the summer, particularly that of a greenhouse, to grow successfully in a relatively short growing season.

In sheltered gardens, it is possible to grow cucumbers and some melons outside, but for intense sweetness, tender fruits, and those that we associate with supermarkets, the greenhouse is the place to grow them. These plants will need a reasonable amount of space and require regular tying in and training, but it's worth it; the prolific nature of cucumbers and the unrivaled sweetness of a warm melon are hard to beat.

Both cucumbers and melons need ample space to grow, as well as warmth and humidity.

Propagation

Cucumbers and melons should be grown from seed. Wait until April to sow them, as they detest the cold and lower light levels of late winter and early spring. These plants grow quickly, and by waiting until conditions are more favorable, you will achieve a strong young plant without the need to nurse it through those duller weeks and months.

Cucumber seeds are generally available as all-female varieties, which will produce fruits that develop behind the female flower. These don't have the bitterness of some of the older types, which is a result of fertilization.

Both cucumber and melon seeds will require heat to germinate, so they are best placed in a heated propagator. The seedlings are particularly sensitive to cold temperatures and should be protected as they develop. Keep them in the heated propagator until uniform germination has occurred, then remove the lid but keep the basal heat on during the day. At night, replace the lid to maintain a more ambient temperature, or bring the plants inside your home to protect them until the next morning.

I sow in pairs and tend to leave both seedlings growing in the pot until early May due to their sensitivity to cold temperatures. At this point, when they are more robust, I cut one seedling off at the base with scissors (this causes less root disturbance than pulling it out), allowing the other to develop on its own. This young plant should not require potting on before planting into its final position.

Growing from seed

The sowing method is the same for both cucumbers and melons—see below.

Instructions

01
Fill a 2¾in (7cm) or 3½in (9cm) pot with peat-free medium, using a tamper or the base of another pot to level and firm the surface.

02
Water well to saturate the potting mix, which avoids unnecessary watering when the seeds begin to germinate.

03
Place two seeds on their sides in the center of the pot and push into the medium by ½in (1cm) to slightly bury them below the surface. Placing the seeds on their side avoids rotting and so reduces the risk of no germination.

04
Cover the large seeds with more medium to the top of the pot.

01

02

03

04

Planting

Wait until mid-May to plant out in your unheated greenhouse, when conditions are a bit more favorable. Both cucumbers and melons require space, and when grown as cordons (see right), they should be planted at least 16in (40cm) apart. A reasonable peat-free potting mix will suffice in containers or grow bags, with supplementary feeding. Greenhouse borders or raised beds should be enriched with well-rotted compost before planting. Most standard grow bags will accommodate two plants per bag, which allows plenty of air circulation between the plants.

Cucumbers are vigorous climbers and are well suited to growing as cordons.

Caring for the crop

These plants are vigorous growers if well looked after. You'll notice that melon plants are a little slower to grow than most cucumbers, but be patient–they get there in the end.

Feeding

From the beginning of May, feed your cucumber and melon plants with a weekly seaweed fertilizer and continue until around mid-June. At this point, several flowers will appear on a strong framework, so start to give a potash-based feed once a week instead, as this encourages the development of more fruit and flowers. If productivity starts to reduce or foliage begins to yellow, add a seaweed feed to your weekly routine. Continue until the frosts or until your plants cease to be productive due to the colder night temperatures of fall.

Training cucumbers

My favorite way to grow greenhouse cucumbers is as a cordon. This involves training a single stem, often up a piece of string, by twisting the plant around the support between each leaf as it grows. Side shoots will develop from the leaf axils and produce flowers, where the immature cucumber develops. The shoots will continue to grow but should be cut off two leaves beyond the developing cucumber, which concentrates energy on fruit production and maintains the shape of the cordon, in turn increasing air movement and reducing the chance of powdery mildew. There are many lunchbox-style or mini cucumbers available now that don't require you to manage their side shoots, as they can support much smaller fruits.

Cordon cucumbers will grow to around 10ft (3m) in height and will keep producing fruit as the plant grows, as long as the temperatures are warm enough and there is sufficient food and water available. Continue growing for as long as conditions are favorable, but if this is not practical, snip out the growing tip when the cucumber reaches the extent of your support.

Tie in melon side shoots and pinch out when they have produced five leaves. Flowers will develop close to the main stem.

Training melons

Melons can be grown along the ground with little training but are harder to manage as a crop. Growing them as cordons allows for more plants in one space, with plenty of air movement for healthy growth and more fruits. They need plenty of space to grow, as we want to encourage the side shoots to develop fruits, which grow horizontally from the main stem. Train a single stem up a piece of string, then attach some horizontal string or wire every 12in (30cm) along the sides of the greenhouse to support the side shoots. As melons need width to grow, give each plant approximately 3ft (1m) of space. Two different varieties can be grown in a smaller space; you just have to be selective in which side shoots you train–for example, one side shoot from a left-hand plant on the first horizontal wire, then the next side shoot from the right-hand plant on the next wire up, alternating as you go.

Encourage a single stem of your melon to the top of your support, the height of which will often be dictated by the size of your greenhouse or the framework you set up. As that main stem develops, tie in the side shoots and stop them by removing the tip when they have produced five leaves. Flowers will develop on secondary shoots from that side shoot of five leaves, close to the main stem. Once you can see melons developing on that secondary side shoot, stop any other further shoots. Melon plants can support five fruits over the summer, so once your plant has developed that number at equal stages of development, encourage those and remove any others.

Pollination of melons

It's easy to spot female flowers on your melon plant because immature melons develop behind the flower. To make sure good fertilization takes place and you achieve five fruits of equal size (to avoid one dominating the others), take a soft paintbrush and gather as much pollen as possible from the male flowers, and expose that to the female flowers, ideally in the heat of the day to help the process.

Aid fertilization for good-quality melons by using a paintbrush to pollinate the flowers.

It's harvest time when melons smell sweet and cucumbers reach 12in (30cm) long.

A seed bath filled with water can act as a reservoir to maintain humidity among your cucumber and melon plants.

Pests and diseases

Both cucumbers and melons can suffer from whitefly and powdery mildew. Monitor whitefly populations and spray with an oil- or soap-based solution or insecticidal soap once a week until populations are under control.

Drier conditions will encourage powdery mildew, particularly on the lower leaves—these plants enjoy a warm, humid environment—so damp down your greenhouse on warm days (see page 114) and maintain that high level of humidity throughout the summer. You may still experience some deterioration or powdery mildew on the lower leaves, which can simply be cut back to encourage more air movement, as most of the growing takes place near the shoot tips.

Harvesting

Keep harvesting cucumbers as they become ripe to encourage more flowers and more fruit to set.

With standard greenhouse cucumbers, the ideal time to harvest is when they reach a length of approximately 12in (30cm). Try to avoid those fruits becoming overdeveloped, as they will lose firmness and sweetness. If in doubt, always pick cucumbers on the slightly immature side for the best eating.

When it comes to harvesting melons, your senses come into play: They often give off a sweet scent when they are ready to harvest. Additionally, when ripe, their flesh tends to have a bit more give when squeezed.

Calendar

January	-
February	-
March	-
April	Sow seeds
May	Reduce to one seedling, pot on, and plant out to final position
June	Train
July	Continue to tie in and harvest
August	Harvest
September	Harvest
October	-
November	-
December	-

Recommended cultivars

Cucumbers

'Carmen' An all-female, popular cultivar due to its prolific nature and disease resistance. Glossy, straight, dark-green fruits.

'Mini Munch' All-female variety that produces snack-sized fruits (ideal for children), which should be picked when around 2¾in (7cm) long. There's no need to manage side shoots.

'Telegraph Improved' An old, all-female cultivar but still popular due to the reliable production of dark-skinned, mild-flavored fruits.

Melons

'Giallo da Inverno' Vigorous, yellow-skinned melon that matures in late summer, with sweet, perfumed flesh. A productive plant, good for melon first-timers.

'Honey Bun' Honeydew type with pale-green, distinctly flavored flesh. This particular cultivar responds well to greenhouse conditions in cooler climates, compared to other honeydew types.

'Sweetheart' Cantaloupe type with sweet, orange flesh. Medium-sized fruit and grows quickly, so it's suitable for greenhouses in cooler climates.

Try melons such as 'Giallo da Inverno' and 'Honey Bun'.

Potatoes

Freshly dug new potatoes are a treat and can be easily grown in bags or large containers. They will also benefit from the extra protection and warmth that a greenhouse provides.

Growing seed potatoes in peat-free potting mix, in good light, and never allowing them to dry out will offer the perfect conditions for a crop of great spuds. When grown in the greenhouse, you will get an earlier crop, and the flavor will have an intensity that can't be rivaled by supermarket produce.

Chitting

Chitting seed potatoes involves encouraging them to produce stubby growths before planting for a more quickly maturing crop. There is a lot of debate about the benefits, and indeed necessity, of chitting potatoes. In all honesty, it is not essential, but in my experience, it gives them a head start, allowing us to harvest a little earlier. It's also useful to see sprouts when planting to ascertain that the potatoes are viable and to indicate the planting direction, with the shoots facing upward.

It is best to start chitting your potatoes as soon as you get them home. You can buy seed potatoes from early January, when the best selection is available. These have been specifically grown for planting, to multiply and mature in the ground, and are not for cooking or eating in their current state. You can plant potatoes from a supermarket, but bear in mind that the crop is often disappointing, though still edible.

Seed potatoes need a frost-free, cool, bright position to achieve dark-green, stumpy shoots. If you've chitted potatoes in the past that resembled an octopus or some sort of alien life form with wayward, long shoots, your room was probably too warm and/or too dark. A spot on a porch or windowsill is ideal for this method. Sprouts should appear within a month, but if the seed potato is firm with no sprouts after four weeks, don't worry—those shoots will soon appear.

You can use an egg carton or seed trays to keep the potatoes in for this process. Look out for the buds, which are small, raised areas, sometimes known as eyes or roses. Position the part of the potato with the most eyes facing upward; the heel of the potato, which is often the narrow end, should be facing downward.

Sprouts should appear on seed potatoes in about four weeks if kept in a cool, bright spot.

Growing potatoes

Potatoes can be planted in a container or grow bag from the middle to the end of March.

01
Half fill a potato bag or container around 20in (50cm) in diameter and depth with plenty of peat-free potting mix.

02
Place three seed potatoes in a triangle, with their sprouts facing up, on the surface of the potting mix.

03
Cover the seed potatoes with 2-4in (5-10cm) of potting mix. When five leaves appear from each seed potato, cover with more potting mix until the leaves are buried.

04
Continue to cover the foliage when five leaves appear until the potting mix reaches the top of the pot or bag. Keep in the protection of your greenhouse until the middle of May, then place outside.

05
Keep moist but not overly wet to avoid rotting during their growing period. Feed weekly with a seaweed or nettle fertilizer (see page 82) to boost growth and yield. The potatoes should be ready to harvest 12 weeks after planting.

01
02
03
04

05

Sweet potatoes

Sweet potatoes are tropical climbing plants that adore the heat of a greenhouse and can be harvested four to five months after planting. Either grown up a set of bamboo canes or allowed to scramble over a membrane, this is an easy-to-grow vegetable that delivers a delicious crop at the end of the summer.

Sweet potatoes are one of those crops that I've become increasingly excited about in recent years due to their suitability for growing under glass and how surprisingly easy they are to propagate. They require very little interference and are incredibly rewarding. Modern cultivars are now widely available and reliable in a variety of conditions. Supermarket-grown tubers are more variable but still easy to grow and lots of fun.

Propagation

Sweet potatoes are propagated via rooted slips. Slips are long shoots that have been removed from a sprouted sweet potato and will root readily from the base when the shoot is submerged in water. Rooted slips are available to buy online from April onward and can be potted up as soon as they arrive through your door. Alternatively, it is possible to grow your own from a tuber bought from a supermarket (see opposite). It is worth bearing in mind, however, that supermarket tubers may be less suited to cooler climates and may need longer to produce a reasonable crop.

Sweet potatoes are best grown as climbers (far left) to keep leaf nodes away from the soil, where they will root.

Sweet potato flowers (left) are a rare but lovely treat in spring or summer.

Instructions

01
Place a tuber in a glass of water with the pointed end facing up and the bottom half immersed in water. Push a metal skewer through it to hold it in position. Place in a heated propagator or on a sunny windowsill while slips develop. Replace the water every few days to prevent bacteria from building up and causing the tuber to deteriorate.

02
Once the tuber has sprouted and shoots have grown to 2–4in (5–10cm), gently remove them, detaching a piece of tuber with the cutting. With most shoots, you can do this using your fingers, but use a knife if the slip does not come away easily.

03
Place the cuttings in a glass of water and leave until roots have formed at the base. Replace the water every few days to prevent bacteria build-up.

04
After a few weeks, the cuttings should have developed a strong root system, indicating that they are ready to be potted up.

05
Pot up the rooted cuttings into individual 2¾in (7cm) pots filled with peat-free potting mix.

01

02

03

04

05

Pot on young plants (top) if roots outgrow their pot.

Plant out into their final position with cane supports (above).

Tie in shoots (left) as they climb the canes.

Planting

Young sweet potato plants should be kept in a warm environment–such as a frost-free greenhouse or heated propagator with the lid removed–until the middle of May, when, once acclimatized, they can be planted into their final position. If roots emerge out of the small pots before the middle of May, when temperatures will be too cold to sustain the plants, pot on to a container that's twice the size to keep them developing strongly.

A large container of peat-free potting mix, a grow bag, or a raised bed will suffice: I would suggest one plant per grow bag, three plants in a 20in (50cm) diameter container, or one plant per 11ft^2 (1m^2) of soil in a raised bed.

Caring for the crop

The growing season for a reasonable crop of sweet potatoes is short and will come to an end in the fall, when light levels and temperatures fall, so a warm, sunny spot in the greenhouse is best.

Watering and feeding

Apply a weekly seaweed-based fertilizer during the growing season. Continue feeding all the way through until harvest to promote lots of healthy growth. Do not allow the soil to dry out, as the tubers require plenty of moisture to swell.

Training

The most important factor when growing sweet potatoes is not to allow the nodes or leaf joints to encounter the soil, as they will root and produce lots of small potatoes, preventing the development of more substantial tubers. Growing sweet potatoes as a climber is more space-efficient, but if you wish to grow them along the ground, do so through landscape fabric to prevent rooting along the stems. The only potatoes that you want to encourage are those attached to the original plant.

Sweet potatoes can be trained up bamboo canes approximately 6½ft (2m) in height. Tying in the stems with string prevents them from coming into contact with any soil or compost.

Pests and diseases

Sweet potato plants may be troubled by aphids, whitefly, and red spider mites. Check for signs of attack on shoot tips and spray with an oil- or soap-based spray or insecticidal soap once a week until populations are under control. Extra humidity by damping down (see page 114) will help reduce red spider mite issues.

Harvesting

Sweet potatoes can be slow to develop in cool climates and require as long a growing season as we can give them. Harvest in early October or when temperatures drop below 41°F (5°C), as growth slows and foliage begins to yellow. Tip the container out or gently lift the tubers with a fork to harvest.

Harvest tubers by gently lifting from the soil when foliage begins to yellow.

Calendar

January	-
February	Place supermarket or last year's tuber in water in a heated propagator
March	Remove cuttings and root in water when 2-4in (5-10cm)
April	Order slips online (slips that arrive in the mail should be potted immediately and potted on when roots appear at the base of the pot through the drainage holes) Pot up rooted cuttings
May	Plant out young plants into final position Feed weekly until harvest with a seaweed-based fertilizer
June	Tie in shoots to avoid foliage encountering the soil
July	Continue to tie in shoots
August	Continue to tie in shoots
September	Continue to tie in shoots
October	Bring indoors to overwinter Harvest
November	Harvest
December	-

Recommended cultivars

'Beauregard Improved' A hardy variety compared to supermarket tubers, which is more reliable when grown in cooler temperatures. The orange-fleshed tubers have a good flavor.
'Bonita' A popular, pale-fleshed sweet potato that is widely available and suitable for greenhouse growing. Tubers have a slightly nutty flavor.
'Evangeline' Requires more warmth than other sweet potatoes, but when given those conditions, it produces an incredibly sweet tuber unrivaled by other widely available cultivars.

Lemongrass

This tropical herb adores the heat of a greenhouse during the summer. The citrus-flavored stems can be used in Asian food and curries, and the leaves make a delicious tea. Plants must be moved into a bright room in the house during the winter.

When we're choosing which foods to grow in our greenhouses, lemongrass probably isn't one of the crops that instantly springs to mind. Having grown this tender herb for several years with great success, however, it has become as much a part of my summer greenhouse cropping as tomatoes, cucumbers, and peppers.

Propagation

There are two easy ways to grow lemongrass: either from seed or by rooting stems purchased from the supermarket. If you can overwinter a clump of lemongrass in a frost-free place with good light levels, division is also possible in the spring, but overwintering this herb can be challenging, so propagating it by seed or stems in the late winter when temperatures start to warm up is a more straightforward method.

Growing from seed

Lemongrass seed is widely available to buy. Start sowing in February (see opposite for sowing instructions) to give your lemongrass plants as long a growing season as possible to achieve the biggest specimens. The cooler the greenhouse environment, the slower your plants will develop, but once the early summer warmth arrives, growth will be far more rapid and you will be treated to a mass of green shoots.

Harvest the lush stems of lemongrass to encourage even more shoots.

Instructions

01
Sow your seeds on a level surface of moist peat-free medium in a 3½in (9cm) pot.

02
Label and cover with enough vermiculite or sieved compost to barely hide the seed, then place in a heated propagator until uniform germination has occurred. Gently acclimatize the seedlings to frost-free greenhouse conditions by initially removing the lid of the propagator (keeping it plugged in) and, once they have adapted to the cooler temperatures, remove the pot.

03
When your seedlings are large enough to handle, prick them out into cell trays. Once established, pot them on into individual 3½in (9cm) pots. Plant into their final position around the middle of May.

01

02

03

Growing from supermarket stems

Store-bought lemongrass stems will root quickly if placed in a glass of water in a heated propagator. The basal plate at the bottom of the stem is where the roots will appear. Change the water in the glass every few days to prevent bacteria from building up and causing rot. Once the stems have a reasonable amount of root, pot up into 3½in (9cm) containers of peat-free potting mix and grow on until roots appear through the drainage holes. Plant out into their final position around mid-May.

Supermarket stems can be rooted in water before potting up.

Plant up three to five plants in a 12in (30cm) container and harvest regularly.

Planting

Whether you have grown your lemongrass from seed or by rooting stems, young plants will be equally happy in containers, grow bags, or borders in your greenhouse, where the extra warmth will accelerate growth and give you a much greater crop. Plants grown from seed in favorable conditions can grow big, up to 4ft (1.2m) in height. I tend to plant three or five in a pot that has a diameter of approximately 12in (30cm) and harvest regularly; the competition within the pot will slow growth, but that pot will be fuller more quickly. Lemongrass grown from a stem tends to have broader foliage as well as thicker stems and is at home in a more congested container, but also when planted individually, due to the lack of competition for food and nutrients.

Caring for the crop

Lemongrass plants are relatively easy to look after, requiring fairly minimal attention. For buoyant growth, however, don't allow the potting mix to dry out and avoid overwatering, which may cause waterlogging and root deterioration.

Feeding

As soon as your young lemongrass plants have established in their 3½in (9cm) pots, they should be fed once a week with a seaweed-based fertilizer to promote strong growth until harvesting at the end of the growing season. The growth we want to promote is foliage and stems, so a balanced feed such as nettle fertilizer (see page 82) or a seaweed-based fertilizer is preferable to a high-potash feed, which promotes fruit and flowers.

Training

Very little training is required for lemongrass. Simply remove dead or dying foliage as it appears around the edges of the clumps to maintain good air movement. Regular feeding will encourage new growth, as will regular harvesting.

Pests and diseases

Lemongrass is relatively pest and disease free, but check for any signs of aphids, particularly on new shoots, and spray weekly with a soap- or oil-based spray until any populations are under control.

Harvesting

Harvest stems when they are large enough to be used in the kitchen (around pencil thickness). These plants grow quickly and the growing season is relatively short, so it is worth making the most of your lemongrass as soon as you can harvest it, which will encourage new shoots. Grazing on this plant is much better than waiting for an ultimate harvest at the end of the season.

Calendar

January	-
February	Sow seeds and/or root stems
March	Prick out and pot on young plants
April	Begin feeding once a week with a seaweed fertilizer
May	Plant out rooted, 3½in (9cm) plants into their final position
June	Continue feeding
July	Harvest stems when at pencil thickness
August	Harvest
September	Harvest
October	Harvest
November	Overwinter clump indoors until March
December	-

Recommended cultivars

Lemongrass is available as *Cymbopogon citratus*, with no widely available cultivars or improvements to the species, although you may occasionally see the more compact *Cymbopogon flexuosus*. Buy seed from a reputable supplier and you can't go too far wrong. Supermarket lemongrass will be more variable, as it's imported from warmer climates.

Ginger

I love to grow ginger in my greenhouse. I get a tremendous amount of joy from growing something a little bit different, which is incredibly easy to buy and then grow, at very little cost.

Ginger is grown as a root vegetable for its culinary uses and anti-inflammatory properties. This tender vegetable loves the heat of the greenhouse in the summer and can be overwintered in the house, until greenhouse conditions are more favorable again.

Propagation

Ginger root is widely available to buy in supermarkets, usually in the fruit and vegetable section. Follow the steps below to propagate your own ginger plant from a store-bought root.

Instructions

01

Select a large ginger root that is firm—softness in any part may lead to rot. Look out for nodules or eyes along the root, as this is where leaves and developing stems will originate.

02

Wash the root under a faucet or in a bowl of water to remove any chemical residue present designed to prevent the ginger root from shooting prematurely; this may be beneficial for supermarkets to prolong the root's shelf life, but for gardeners, it can slow down the rooting and growing process.

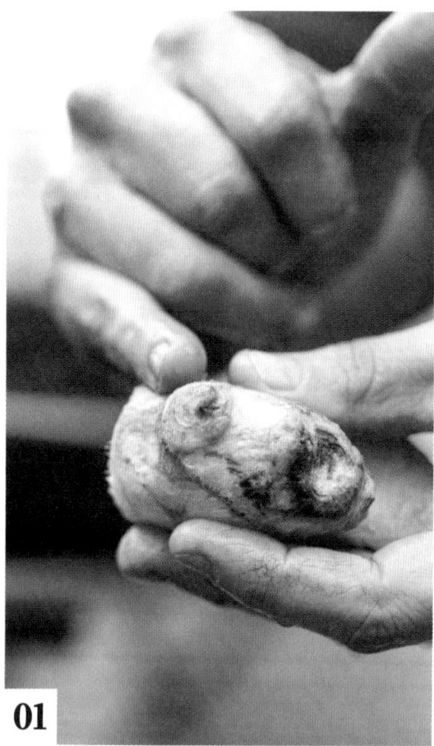

01

02

03

04

05

03
Fill a seed tray with peat-free potting mix to the top, then part-bury the ginger root in the soil. Leave the top half exposed.

04
Water thoroughly.

05
Place in a heated propagator, exposing the root to reasonable light levels but keeping it out of direct light. If you do not have a heated propagator, place the seed tray in a clear plastic bag and position on a well-lit windowsill. The extra humidity will promote growth and a heated environment will accelerate the growing process. Ginger grown in a clear plastic bag will still perform, albeit a little more slowly.

Planting

Once your ginger has produced a shoot that is around 2in (5cm) in length, usually six weeks after it was planted (depending on the level of warmth), it is ready to be potted up. The root will grow across the surface of the soil throughout the summer, so use a container that allows for 4in (10cm) of growth from the edge of the root to the edge of the pot all the way around. The pot should be of a reasonable depth, 6in (15cm) or so, but most of the growth will be along the surface.

Pot up using a peat-free potting mix, maintaining the depth of the root as in the original seed tray, and water well. Your young ginger plant needs to be kept moist but not overly wet to grow happily.

In cooler climates, ginger likes a sunny, warm spot. In very high temperatures, however, it will benefit from some partial shade.

Ginger does best grown in individual pots in a warm greenhouse atmosphere.

Cold, waterlogged conditions will be detrimental to growth, so water sparingly until the early summer when it can become more regular, around two or three times a week.

Growing ginger in pots gives the best results, as the growing plants are more responsive to fertilizer and rooting in the peat-free medium. Free-draining, bright raised beds or borders in the greenhouse can work well, too, but ensure that the ginger plants are not overshadowed by other plant canopies.

Caring for the crop

With ginger, we want to achieve consistent growth throughout the summer, ensuring good root development and strong shoots.

Feeding

Once potted into its final position, and when the ambient warmth and light levels increase in the greenhouse, usually at the end of May, feed your

Check moisture levels in the soil before watering ginger to avoid waterlogging.

Calendar

January	Overwinter inside
February	Overwinter inside
March	Overwinter inside
April	Overwinter inside
May	Acclimatize to the greenhouse, feed weekly
June	Feed weekly with a seaweed fertilizer
July	Continue feeding
August	Continue feeding
September	Continue feeding
October	Harvest, divide, repot
November	Overwinter inside
December	Overwinter inside

ginger root once a week with a seaweed-based fertilizer until the end of September, when the root can be harvested.

Training

Very little training is required as your ginger grows throughout the summer. Simply remove any dead or dying leaves to maintain good air circulation and healthy growth. If your ginger root grows quickly and reaches the edge of its existing container, repot into a slightly larger container to allow for more growth.

Pest and disease

I find growing ginger relatively trouble free, with few pests and diseases, although the usual suspects of aphids and mealybugs may cause you a problem. If populations of these sap-sucking pests build up, a weekly spray of insecticidal soap or physically removing them with your thumb and forefinger will reduce levels to a manageable amount.

Harvesting

Given warm and dappled light conditions throughout the summer, your ginger root will be ready to harvest in the fall. As the evenings become colder and the nights get longer, the growth rate of the root will slow right down. It is unlikely that it will grow much more through the fall and winter, so most people harvest ginger at the beginning of fall.

To continue the process, retain and pot up some suitable sections of root to be brought inside. Place on a sunny windowsill in a frost-free room to keep them alive during the winter, ready to start growing again the following spring.

Recommended cultivars

It is most likely that you will source your ginger root from a supermarket. The largest, plumpest roots with many nodes or eyes on them will give you the best chance of success. There are no widely available ginger cultivars for gardeners, though that may change in the future.

Strawberries

Winter and early spring can be challenging when it comes to deciding what crops we can grow in our greenhouses, but delicious, jewel-bright strawberries grown in raised beds, containers, or hanging baskets are a must-have for every gardener.

Set your hanging basket inside a terracotta pot to plant up. A standard basket can fit four strawberry plants around the edge and one in the center.

There's nothing like a ripe strawberry, fresh and warmed by the sun from your greenhouse in the early summer. The protection and extra warmth that your greenhouse provides will encourage an earlier crop than we can expect from our gardens. A hanging basket that contains five strawberry plants will be enough to either offer you a regular treat or something more substantial.

Propagation

From June onward, your strawberries should start producing rhizomes on which the runners (young plants) will grow. For the first two years, these runners should be removed, as we want to concentrate the plant's energy on root development and fruit production. Wait until the third year before you start to encourage propagation and the cultivation of the next generation of plants, as older plants tend to be less productive. When this time comes, allow the rhizomes to develop, and when a young strawberry plant begins to form at the end, pin it to the surface of a 3½in (9cm) pot of peat-free potting mix. The contact with the medium will help initiate roots, and once the young plant has established in the pot, it can be detached from the mother plant where it meets the rhizome.

Planting

There are several ways to grow strawberries either in a greenhouse or under a tunnel cloche (see page 32). Young plants are often available in garden centers and nurseries in the fall, so planting at the end of September and early October will allow plants to establish before the worst of the winter weather sets in for fruiting the following summer.

Growing strawberries in a hanging basket makes use of the roof space in your greenhouse and

A hanging basket in the greenhouse keeps fruits away from slugs and snails and allows plants to establish early in the season.

Hang your basket of strawberries at the most convenient height for you to harvest the fruit.

elevates those precious fruits away from many garden pests. The hanging nature of the fruit makes growing them in baskets a great solution for all-around ripening. A 14in (36cm) basket will accommodate five strawberry plants. Position four around the very edge of the basket to encourage a more trailing habit and one in the center. Any peat-free potting mix will be suitable, with supplementary feeding required as the plants establish and grow.

Tunnel cloches should be 12in (30cm) high and 2ft (60cm) wide to accommodate a row of strawberries in the open ground and allow plenty of air movement. Strawberries will grow well in fertile, free-draining soil in a sunny position. Before planting, spread a 2in (5cm) layer of well-rotted manure or garden compost on the surface of the soil, then lightly fork it in to add fertility and help young plants establish. Plant your strawberries

Calendar

January	Minimal watering
February	Increase watering and weekly seaweed feed until fruit set
March	Ventilate when warm
April	Ventilate when warm; monitor pollination
May	Harvest
June	Harvest
July	Remove runners on first- and second-year plants
August	-
September	Plant up
October	Plant up
November	Minimal watering
December	Minimal watering

Strawberries are versatile plants; they will be happy growing in containers, beds, hanging baskets, under cloches, and in grow bags.

12in (30cm) apart and water well, making sure that they do not dry out underneath the polyethylene. Raising the sides of the cloche on warm days will improve ventilation and allow pollinators to access your strawberry flowers. Once the fruit begins to form, add a layer of dry straw underneath the fruit to protect it from the damp soil and reduce rotting.

Watering and feeding

Greenhouse- or cloche-grown strawberries will need our intervention to provide enough water to meet their needs. Do not overwater during the winter—just provide enough to prevent the leaves from wilting through drought. Watering should increase as the fruit begins to set. There are no hard and fast rules for watering because small plants in low temperatures and dull light conditions require very little, while more frequent watering is needed when temperatures are high and the fruit is swelling. If in doubt, water a little less and more frequently, as overwatering will cause rot and the leaching of nutrients from the potting mix.

Similarly, too much fertilizer can reduce the plants' fruit production by encouraging lots of foliage and fewer flowers. Most peat-free potting mixes will contain sufficient fertilizer to last between four and six weeks. However, although strawberries will grow very little during the winter, when light levels and temperatures increase in February and beyond, a weekly seaweed feed will be of great benefit in containers, baskets, beds, and under cloches.

Training

Strawberries require little attention through the winter, besides removing dead or damaged foliage. On those warm, sunny winter days, if the temperature inside the greenhouse starts to increase to 59–68°F (15–20°C), make sure the space around your strawberries is well ventilated with plenty of air movement. In an unheated greenhouse, I would expect strawberries to come into flower around the end of April and the berries to ripen four to six weeks beyond that. Providing lots of ventilation during those warm days is also important to allow pollinators to access the flowers to ensure a reasonable crop. If you are concerned that there are few pollinating insects around, lightly brush a soft paintbrush over the flowers and move between anthers and stigmas of different strawberry flowers to replicate the action of pollinators.

Pests and diseases

For healthy strawberry plants through the winter, remove dead and withered leaves and keep the soil free from weeds. Keep an eye on the undersides of leaves and shoot tips to monitor for aphids, and either physically remove them or apply insecticidal soap at weekly intervals until the populations are under control.

Vine weevil can be a danger when growing strawberries; they are particularly fond of the fruits and are more prevalent in wet soil, so allowing your potting mix to dry out slightly between waterings will help reduce the risk. Wilting foliage maybe a sign that vine weevil larvae are present in your container or basket. Biological controls are available for the larvae in the spring if infestations are caught early. Extensive damage can be difficult to recover from, and in some cases composting the plants is best.

Botrytis or gray mold and rot also need to be managed when growing strawberries. Increase air movement and remove dead and dying leaves, as they appear to keep these issues under control.

Slugs and snails are a concern, too, and can be dealt with through organic means with beer traps and upturned grapefruit skins. Child- and pet-friendly pellets are also available. Of course, by planting strawberries in a hanging basket, you can avoid issues with slugs.

Harvesting

Outdoors, the strawberry season typically starts around late April to May in the south and around late May to June in the north; nationally, however, the season can start as early as January. Plants that are grown in greenhouses, either unheated or heated enough to protect the plants from frost, will fruit around four weeks earlier than those in the garden, while those under tunnel cloches will produce fruit approximately two weeks before those in the garden.

Once harvested, those plants that have been grown in a hanging basket can be planted out into a strawberry bed in the garden to crop for another couple years. After that time, runners can be propagated from those plants to produce another generation. Those strawberries that have been grown under a cloche can be treated as garden strawberries for the next couple years, with the polyethylene removed after cropping.

Recommended cultivars for early cropping

'Cambridge Favourite' One of the most widely grown, as it is one of the most reliable croppers. Fruits hang on the plant for a long time and maintain their freshness. They are medium-sized, with some disease resistance and good flavor.

'Cambridge Vigour' Produces large conical fruits in the first year, which ripen early and are a joyful scarlet color with a firm flesh and good flavor. Several trusses of fruit are produced in that first year.

'Red Gauntlet' Heavy-cropping, bearing large, rounded fruits. Fruiting is early in the first year and slightly later in the second and third. Perfect for growing under glass and cloches, and can sometimes produce a second crop in late summer. Reasonable disease resistance and good flavor.

'Cambridge Favourite' is a favorite for a reason. Reliable, disease resistant, and delicious, it's a great choice for a hanging basket.

Peaches and apricots

You don't need to have an enormous Victorian greenhouse to grow apricot or peach trees successfully. Many modern cultivars are compact and can be grown in containers, making it easy to bring them into your greenhouse over the winter to give them a degree of protection.

Unless you have an incredibly sheltered garden, to get the best from these trees, they need a little protection from the winter wet, and particularly in the early spring, to prevent disease and to provide a more effective environment for pollination. Peaches and apricots are accustomed to a cold winter but not a wet one. An unheated greenhouse is a perfect place to overwinter them before moving them outside in May until leaf fall.

Grafting explained

The top growth, or the scion wood, is the fruiting part of the tree and has been selected for its productivity, taste, and disease resistance. The rootstock onto which the fruiting part of the tree is grafted will govern the vigor of the tree. To grow an apricot or peach in a pot requires a rootstock that will produce a compact tree for the best results.

Propagation

Although it is possible to grow apricots and peaches from seed, it is unlikely that the plant will produce fruit of a reasonable quality and quantity. To get the best results, source your tree from a reputable nursery, where it will have been grafted onto a suitable rootstock. A number of cultivars will be available within a patio range of trees, but ensure that the rootstock will produce a compact tree suitable for a container in the longer term.

Planting

It is best to plant your tree from November to March, when it is dormant, without any leaves. Planting in this state often leads to better establishment and less stress for the tree. When planting apricots and peaches either in the ground or in a container, good drainage is essential. In a container, ensure that there are adequate drainage holes at the base of the pot and incorporate several handfuls of coarse sand into the peat-free potting mix.

Instructions

01
Ensure that there is a good layer of broken terracotta or stones at the base of the pot to keep the drainage hole(s) clear of soil so water can escape. Peaches and apricots need sharp drainage without a waterlogged root ball, especially during the winter.

02
Half-fill the container with peat-free potting mix and incorporate a few handfuls of sand for additional drainage.

03
Remove the tree from its pot and gently tease out the roots for better establishment.

04
Plant the tree at the same level in the new pot as it was in the original pot from the nursery.

05
Fill in around the root ball with potting mix, avoiding air pockets, which will deter root growth.

06
Firm in well all around the root ball and water generously to help settle the potting mix.

Caring for the crop

Apricots and peaches are most commonly grown as standard trees and will require a little shaping.

Feeding and watering

During the first year, from early March until the end of September, a weekly liquid feed of a seaweed-based fertilizer will ensure healthy, all-around growth as the tree establishes. When the tree is in full leaf water regularly, but as the leaves change color in fall, reduce watering and keep the root ball on the drier side. Water sparingly during winter merely to keep the tree alive, as excess water will lead to root rot. In the late winter of year two, and then each year after, remove the top 2in (5cm) of potting mix and replace with fresh peat-free mix to invigorate the roots and boost fertility. As the tree breaks into flower and leaf, increase watering gradually and begin the weekly feeding in early March.

Training

As your tree grows, begin to gently sculpt it into a symmetrical shape, reducing any dominant shoots to within the canopy. Any dead, diseased, or damaged stems should be removed to the point of fresh, healthy growth. Only prune apricot and peach trees while they are actively growing (March to September) to avoid silver leaf disease, which is more prevalent during the winter months and enters the tree via wounds. Pruning should be minimal, as the vigor of the tree is managed by the dwarfing rootstock. Make small adjustments to maintain a pleasing shape, and avoid any major limb removal. Do not expose the tree to frosts, and keep it in the greenhouse until mid-May.

Apricots and peaches will flower under glass in February and March. There are few pollinators

Hand-pollinate apricot and peach blossom, as pollinators are scarce when it blooms.

Train a tree into a fan

Apricot and peach trees can be trained into a fan over several years, using horizontal support wires 12in (30cm) apart.

Train two side branches along canes at a 40° angle to the wires. Cut out the leader stem, and cut each side branch to 18in (45cm).

Year 1, early spring

In spring, prune branches by a third. In summer, tie in new shoots to extra canes. Cut back inward-/outward-facing shoots and fruits.

Year 2, early spring and summer

Cut back main branches by a quarter in spring. Reduce overcrowded side shoots. Continue to tie in wanted growth to canes.

Year 3, early spring and summer

around at this time of year, so take a soft paintbrush and transfer pollen from one flower to another to fertilize them, leading to fruit. This should be done a few times during the flowering period of your tree.

When fruit has set in April, thin to around 4in (10cm) apart to avoid overburdening your tree and to help produce reasonable-sized fruit.

Pests and diseases

Aphids and red spider mites are likely when growing stone fruit under glass, but these pests are reduced in number by exposing them to the outdoor conditions during the summer. Higher humidity will deter red spider mites and physical removal, or a weekly spray of insecticidal soap, will reduce populations. Die-back can occur on occasion, but minimal pruning will reduce the risk.

To train trees into a fan, tie in branches and clip into shape.

Recommended cultivars

- **Sibley's Patio Apricot 'Tomcot'** An outstanding cultivar for both heavy cropping and reliability. This patio version has been developed not to exceed 4ft (1.2m) in height.
- **Sibley's Patio Peach 'Peregrine'** Fruits have white flesh, which is sweet and juicy, and most importantly, the tree fruits reliably. With gentle pruning, the tree should not exceed 4ft (1.2m) in height.

Apricot 'Tomcot' produces an abundant crop of beautifully formed fruits for harvest from July.

Harvesting

Both peaches and apricots will become soft on the tree before they are ripe. There should be a general sweet scent in the air or around the fruit when ripe. A few fallen fruits around the base of the tree are also a good indication that they are ready to pick. Fruits should be harvested around July and are well colored when ripe.

Calendar

January	Do not prune
February	Pollinate flowers
March	Pollinate flowers and begin feeding
April	Thin fruit
May	Continue feeding and watering
June	Feed and water
July	Harvest
August	Harvest
September	Feed and water
October	Stop feeding and reduce watering
November	Do not prune
December	Do not prune

Citrus

Citrus comprises a large group of plants, including lemons, limes, grapefruits, kumquats, oranges, mandarins, clementines, satsumas–the list goes on. Originating in subtropical and tropical regions across Asia and Australia, they love warmth and high humidity and will not tolerate frost, making greenhouse protection a must in cold winters.

To grow citrus trees successfully in cooler climates, generally you need to put them in containers so that they can enjoy the summer outside and then be overwintered inside a greenhouse for that extra protection from temperatures below 41°F (5°C), for the hardiest types.

Propagation

Most citrus trees that will produce fruit successfully in northern European climates will be specific cultivars that have been grafted onto rootstocks, bred to cope with our weather conditions. Although it is perfectly feasible to grow citrus from seeds, it is unlikely the tree will produce fruit.

Planting

The container needs to be of a reasonable size, with drainage holes, and deeper than it is wide, but with a substantial base to provide ballast, preventing the tree from toppling over in the wind. Avoid a container with a wide base and narrow neck, as this will make repotting very difficult without sacrificing the pot. Your citrus tree can survive quite happily with a compact root ball without the need to constantly repot it into a larger container. When the tree begins to lift out of your pot, it's an indication that it needs to move up a pot size.

Citrus fruits develop from the flowers and are slow to ripen, often taking many months.

When repotting or potting up your citrus for the first time, use a potting mix made for citrus, or combine an acidic potting mix with added sand.

Caring for the crop

Key to growing citrus plants is getting the soil balance right, managing feeding and watering, and controlling pests.

Feeding

Citrus trees dislike alkaline soil with a high pH, so they should be watered with rainwater, particularly if you live in an area with hard water. If your tree looks sluggish and does not produce fresh growth or sizable fruit, there may be an issue in iron absorption. A citrus fertilizer should help. Failing that, sulfur chips or flowers of sulfur can be applied to reduce the pH of the growing medium and reinvigorate your tree.

Citrus trees require feeding throughout the year. There are many specialty feeds available online and in garden centers, but principally a high-nitrogen feed during the summer will promote growth and prevent premature fruit drop. During the winter and spring, when blossom and fruit is developing, a balanced fertilizer such as a seaweed liquid feed will supply all the major nutrients to keep your citrus healthy and productive. Most suppliers will offer a winter and summer feed.

Don't let your citrus tree dry out through the growing year. During winter, however, when the tree is exposed to cooler temperatures, growth will slow down or stop, and this means the roots will stop absorbing moisture; if additional water is added, rot and root death may occur. Keep the tree on the drier side during the winter but not completely dry, increasing the amount of water as the plants come into active growth.

Use rainwater to water citrus plants (right), and add sulfur chips to the medium (below) to reduce alkalinity in the soil.

Training

Pruning can be carried out throughout the year to achieve your desired shape, but it is best to do so immediately after fruiting, before the next flush of foliage. Light pruning will encourage branching and prevent long, wayward growth. Cut back to a leaf node, preferably one that is facing in the direction you wish new shoots to grow. Flowers will appear on old and new wood, but shoots at the base of the tree should be removed, as they will be rootstock suckers, which will dominate if allowed to grow. There will be a surge of growth in spring, which is normal. If any stems become dominant and disrupt the shape and symmetry of the tree, gently remove the shoot tip to encourage more branched growth. It is far better to trim annually to gently create a well-shaped tree instead of doing any major pruning, which can leave ugly stumps and thick stems.

Check citrus leaves for pests on a regular basis so preventative measures can be taken as soon as possible.

Pests

There are several pests (see page 124) that can cause problems when growing citrus trees.

Red spider mites

These cause a build-up of sooty mold–a result of the honeydew they produce as they feed on the sap of the tree. Leaves will become mottled and discolored, eventually dropping off. A fine webbing can be a tell-tale sign of the presence of this pest. Biological controls, a weekly preventative spray of insecticidal soap, or placing the plant outside during summer will reduce populations. Washing the leaf surface with warm, soapy water will alleviate the symptoms of the sooty mold.

Whitefly and aphids

The first sign of these pests will be clouds of whitefly as you disturb the foliage or clusters of aphids on the shoot tips and buds. Biological controls, a weekly spray of insecticidal soap, or placing the tree outside in summer will help reduce them.

Mealybug

A sap-sucking insect found under leaves or around leaf joints. Honeydew will be one of the first signs, then cottonlike substances on the leaves or shoot tips, which hide a mass of eggs. This is one of the most difficult pests to deal with in a greenhouse, but by painting neat denatured alcohol onto the insect whenever they are spotted, you will keep populations down. Biological controls are also available, which are particularly effective in a greenhouse environment. A summer vacation outside for your tree will also reduce populations.

Scale insects

Scale insects look pretty different from the other citrus pests but are equally as debilitating and will suck the tree's sap and secrete honeydew, leading to sooty mold. They appear as little brown warts or oval scales around the shoot tips or on leaf and stem surfaces. Larger, adult scale insects can be removed by rubbing them off with your fingers. Applying denatured alcohol with a paintbrush also helps reduce populations.

Vine weevil

The most damaging part of this beetle's life cycle is the grubs in the growing medium, which rapidly eat through roots, particularly the young root tips, causing the tree's foliage to collapse. Biological controls in the form of nematodes are available and should be applied twice a year, in spring and fall, as a preventative. Keeping your citrus on the drier side during winter will help deter vine weevil.

Calendar

January	Winter feeding, harvesting
February	Winter feeding, harvesting
March	Pruning and repotting (if required)
April	Winter feeding
May	Summer feeding
June	Summer feeding, flowering
July	Summer feeding, flowering
August	Summer feeding, flowering
September	Summer feeding
October	Winter feeding
November	Winter feeding, harvesting
December	Winter feeding, harvesting

Recommended cultivars

Citrus × meyeri 'Meyer' AGM A great citrus for beginners or those with more modest facilities, as this lemon will tolerate cooler temperatures and is compact and reliable in its fruit production.

Harvesting

Fruits are generally harvested between October and March but can appear throughout the year. It is unnecessary to thin your citrus fruits, as any surplus that the tree cannot support will be shed naturally.

Flowers

Growing flowers in a greenhouse can feel indulgent, as traditionally growing under glass has served the more practical function of delivering home-grown food. However, to fully utilize your greenhouse throughout the year, there are a number of flowers that can be grown to enhance the beauty of the space or be cut for a vase in the house.

There is a great deal of joy to be had in growing your own cut flowers or flowers to enjoy as part of your greenhouse environment. Spring-flowering bulbs, stocks, anemones, and ranunculus can offer color and scent during the early part of the year, followed by zinnias, marigolds, and tender bulbs through the summer and fall. Space tends to be at a premium during the summer in the greenhouse, with firm favorites such as tomatoes, cucumbers, and peppers taking center stage. But the winter and spring can be seasons where there's more room to play, making the cultivation of flowers for decoration and cutting less of a dilemma.

Winter protection

You can utilize your greenhouse during the winter to protect plants that are tolerant of cooler temperatures but less tolerant of excessive moisture. Fall-planted ranunculus and anemones, for example, will fare far better in a greenhouse; they will grow slowly during the winter, then gather momentum in early spring and be very generous in their succession of flowers until the early summer, when they will make way for summer crops (either edible or ornamental).

Similarly, spring bulbs can become damaged in a garden through heavy rainfall and windy conditions. Growing a number in containers, which can then be transferred into the house or kept stationary to decorate your greenhouse, has the advantage of protecting them within the sheltered environment so the flowers are unspoiled. Some bulbs can also be very short, making it difficult to appreciate the intricacies of the flower when they are so low to the ground. By growing flowers such as crocus, dwarf iris, and miniature daffodils in containers, however, you can elevate them on benching, allowing you to marvel at their complexities and scents at a more comfortable height.

There are a number of beautiful flowers that aren't hardy and require protecting in our greenhouses over the winter from frosts and more extreme weather. Dahlias, pelargoniums, fuchsias,

Easy flowers to grow in your greenhouse

- Hardy spring bulbs (see page 204)
- Young bedding plants in containers and hanging baskets (see page 208)
- Fuchsias and pelargoniums (see page 208)
- Zinnias (see page 202)
- Marigolds
- Anemones (see page 199)

Bulbs, such as mixed daffodils (below) or ranunculus (right), will benefit from the dry protection of a greenhouse.

More advanced

- Ranunculus (see page 199)
- Stocks (see page 200)
- Tender bulbs (see page 204)

and heliotrope can be kept in a near-dormant state through the cold and darker months, ready to be revitalized when conditions become more favorable. Several plants need maintaining with an absence of food and minimal water to overwinter them (see page 196), as any growth is hard to sustain and attractive to pests. It's hard not to intervene and encourage growth during the winter, in these instances, but you'll do more harm than good until the warmer weather arrives.

A head start

Our greenhouses during the winter and early spring can be highly productive, producing several plants that are destined for our gardens or containers but that need the protection of a greenhouse until the conditions outside improve. Using your greenhouse to nurture young plants for containers and baskets or for growing on plants, such as sweet peas and chrysanthemums, for decoration and cut flowers later in the season is to be encouraged and is a far easier process than you might think. Giving young plants the extra protection and warmth of a greenhouse in the early spring will mean that they're more developed, more robust, and likely to come into flower earlier than those grown in cooler conditions or purchased later in the year.

Growing flowers in your greenhouse should never be seen as a cop-out or an indulgent alternative to growing food. One of the most precious things about a greenhouse is that it is your space to grow and nurture plants in the way that you want to, creating an environment that gives you a sense of accomplishment and pleasure. Having a part of your greenhouse dedicated to growing ornamental plants goes a long way to making it a richer and more diverse place.

Tropical plants

Your greenhouse is the perfect place to give extra protection during the early spring to a range of more exotic plants, which will provide a tremendous amount of flower power for your garden or containers during the summer.

If left outside in colder climates, tropical plants such as cannas, bananas, begonias, and dahlias–which originate from warm climates such as South America and Asia, so do not experience a frost in their natural habitat–would likely perish over the winter months. Kept in a frost-free greenhouse, however, this group overwinters in a dormant state before coming into growth earlier in the growing season, resulting in a much bigger and more advanced plant that can be introduced into your garden when the risk of frost has passed.

Cannas

Originating in the Andean region, cannas have a wide range of colorful foliage, which provides interest during late summer, when other plants are slowing down and losing their vibrancy. They can be grown in containers and borders, offering much-needed height at the back of displays.

Cannas can survive brief periods of frost outside in a sheltered and free-draining garden, with the protection of a thick mulch to insulate the roots. To be more certain of bringing them through the winter, however, it is best to lift them before the first frosts and containerize them in peat-free potting mix to overwinter in a frost-free greenhouse. Trim back foliage to 2in (5cm) from the top of the pot, as this will simply die back if left. New shoots will emerge in spring, when watering can increase with growth. Cannas can be acclimatized to cooler weather and then planted out or potted up at the end of May.

Cannas add bold, architectural shape and stunning color to a border or container display for a truly tropical look.

Tip

To improve insulation and increase the ambient temperature via more efficient heating, line the inside of your greenhouse with bubble wrap (see page 66). This will ensure a better success rate of overwintering your tender plants.

Bananas

Originating from the subtropical regions of China, *Musa basjoo*—sometimes known as a hardy banana or Japanese banana—is incredibly exotic looking and adds drama to containers and borders. It can tolerate a frost, but if exposed to regular and more severe frosts, it is likely to either reshoot from the base or die off completely.

To grow a more impressive and statuesque banana plant, it is best to either protect it in place with straw and horticultural fleece if growing outside, or to grow it in a container, or lift and containerize it in the fall (see below), and bring it into your greenhouse just before the first frosts. Your banana will benefit from a greenhouse that is heated just above freezing over winter and early spring. It can then be acclimatized to the outdoor conditions and either planted out or grown in a container outside from the end of May.

Lifting a banana for winter protection

Follow these simple steps if lifting your banana from the soil and containerizing it for overwintering in the greenhouse.

01
Lift each stem with a reasonable root ball that is manageable, then repot into a large container of peat-free potting mix.

02
Water the banana plant enough to settle the potting mix, then trim off any damaged foliage. There will be some die-back during the winter, so any dying foliage should be removed to prevent rot. Fresh growth will then emerge from the center of the plant as the weather warms. Water more regularly in response to the freshly emerging foliage.

01

02

Tuberous begonias

Tuberous begonias are floriferous and work well as single plants in pots or as a great addition to container displays. Unlike many foliage begonias, tuberous types go dormant during winter and can be easily stored in a frost-free greenhouse if kept dry, to be brought back into growth in the spring.

In October, or before the first frosts, bring your tuberous begonia in from your patio and begin the process of drying out the root ball. You'll notice that the foliage begins to yellow as the temperatures drop in the evening; this is a sign that the begonia is beginning its dormancy period. Continuing to water your begonia as it starts to die back will cause rot and root death, so, even though it may feel counterintuitive, withhold water at this stage to prepare your begonia for overwintering.

The fiery flowers of *Begonia boliviensis* 'Bossa Nova Orange' will add flair to any display.

Repotting a begonia

Late February, when your begonia is just beginning to break into growth, is the time to repot. Once done, gradually increase watering with growth, starting with a weekly seaweed fertilizer from April, switching to a high-potash tomato fertilizer when it begins to flower.

01
When you notice buds swell and young shoots begin to emerge from the overwintered tuber, tease the root ball from the pot.

02
Remove the top few centimeters of old potting mix from the surface and around 2in (5cm) from beneath the tuber. This will allow space for fresh potting mix, which will help promote strong growth in spring.

03
Using a clean pot, fill the base with peat-free potting mix, then repot the begonia to the same depth as it was in the previous pot. Avoid planting too deep, as this will cause the stems to rot.

02

01

03

04
Firm the potting mix well, ensuring that no air gaps exist around the root ball, which will hinder future root growth.

05
Water well to settle the potting mix around the begonia. Keep the potting mix moist to support the new growth and place in a frost-free greenhouse. Your begonia can be placed outside after the risk of frosts has passed or kept in your greenhouse as a display plant.

04

05

Dahlias

Dahlias are wonderful flowers to have in the garden and can be grown in a variety of ways. Seed-raised dahlias produce a range of colors through genetic diversity, whereas tubers or cuttings will produce a genetic replica of the parent plant if uniformity or a specific characteristic are desired.

Dahlias are not frost hardy and, to ensure survival, need to be lifted and then repotted to overwinter in a frost-free greenhouse; these plants can then be used to produce cuttings (see overleaf). Some gardeners can overwinter tubers in the ground if they have free-draining soil and use a layer of insulating mulch. In my experience, however, hardiness can be dependent on cultivar, and I often lose around 30 percent of my dahlias when overwintered in the ground. When numbers are modest or I only have a single plant of a particular cultivar, I lift the tuber and overwinter it in a frost-free greenhouse to have a better chance of growing that dahlia the following year. Acclimatize them from mid-May in a cold frame so they are ready to be planted out at the end of the month, when the risk of frost has passed.

Tip

Dahlias are extremely floriferous but will slow down in their flower production if allowed to go to seed. Keep deadheading throughout the summer to ensure a great display until the first frosts.

Dahlias such as 'Carolina Wagemans' will keep on flowering until the frosts.

Lifting and repotting a dahlia tuber

Although dahlias can be overwintered in free-draining soil with a layer of insulating mulch, this method is by no means a guarantee of success. For a greater chance of overwintering your dahlia tubers, lift and repot them for protection in a frost-free greenhouse.

01
Before the first frosts, lift your dahlia plant with a reasonable root ball that contains the tubers. Avoid damaging the tubers as much as possible–the use of a border fork instead of a spade will help.

02
Bring the plant and tuber into your greenhouse or potting shed. Knock off any surplus soil and examine the roots to look for any damage.

03
Trim off any damaged roots or tubers that are likely to rot. Then cut off the top growth, leaving a stem that's around 2in (5cm) in length.

04
Repot into a container that will easily house the tuber without squashing it. Fill the pot with peat-free potting mix so the tuber is just below the surface of the potting mix. This will encourage more cutting if you wish to propagate in a few months' time (see opposite). Water the tuber to settle the potting mix, but then keep it on the dry side until growth emerges in spring. At that stage, increase watering in relation to the amount of growth.

01

02

03

04

Taking dahlia cuttings

Taking softwood, basal cuttings can help you grow far greater numbers of your favorite dahlia.

01
Once your tubers have produced shoots that are around 2in (5cm) long, with a sharp knife, remove the cuttings at the base with a small amount of tuber tissue.

02
Trim any extra pieces of tuber to just below the lowest leaf joint.

03
Trim off the lower leaves, leaving the shoot tip and one or two pairs of leaves at the top.

04
Insert the cutting into a small pot of peat-free potting mix and perlite (a 50:50 mixture will work well) and label the pot. Use a wooden skewer to make the holes in the potting mix to prevent damaging your soft cutting.

05
Place in a heated propagator or on a sunny windowsill, out of direct sunlight, until roots emerge through the drainage holes at the base of the pot.

06
At this point, the cuttings can be potted on individually into peat-free potting mix. Pot on again as they grow, ready for their final destination in the garden or containers at the end of May.

01

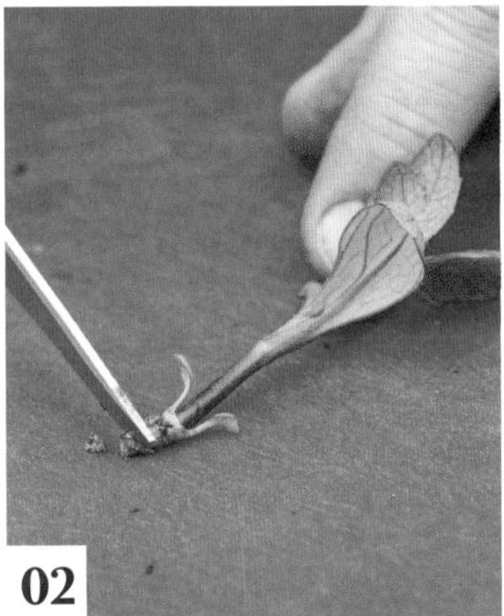

02

03

04

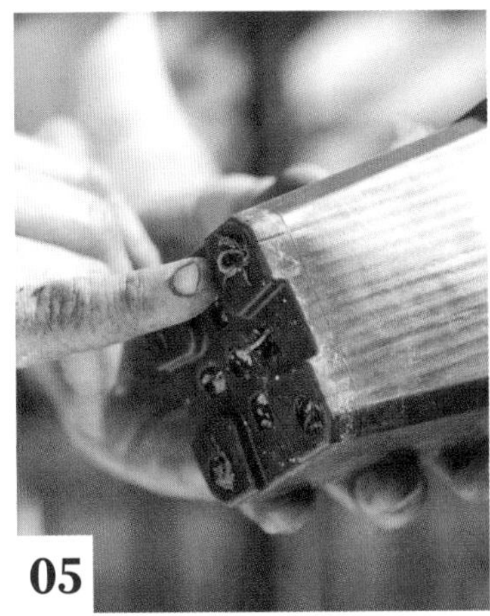

05

06

Overwintering tender plants

Greenhouses give us the ability to grow a far more exotic range of tender plants than we would be able to in our gardens—not least because, by offering extra protection from cold temperatures and excessive winter rainfall, we can nurture these frost-hating plants through the winter.

There may be some very sheltered gardens with free-draining soil that can overwinter tender plants quite happily, but there are no guarantees. Creating a frost-free environment in the greenhouse through insulation and heating will provide the right conditions to successfully overwinter tender plants to ensure another season of healthy, vibrant growth.

When and where to move

As the days begin to shorten and those nighttime temperatures drop, you'll notice that growth rate will slow right down. At this stage, tender plants in the ground need to be lifted, potted up, and brought in (frost or no frost) and container plants moved inside.

There should be no great ambition to actively grow these plants over winter; we are simply keeping them alive until conditions become more favorable. In this state of near dormancy, tender plants require hardly any food and just enough water to sustain them in a frost-free environment.

Freestanding greenhouses, as well as mini lean-to greenhouses, can be used for overwintering and, in the case of plants such as evergreen cacti and succulents, also for creating winter displays.

Overwintered container plants can be relocated outdoors around mid-May.

A greenhouse is the perfect place to overwinter tender succulents, such as aeoniums and echeverias, while keeping them on display.

One of the most common reasons why plants fail to overwinter is excessive watering when plants aren't growing.

Both structures can be heated against frosts and will protect plants from the winter wet while allowing plenty of light transmission during the darker months and into spring. Come the warmer weather, tender container plants, such as pelargoniums and aeoniums, can be brought out of hibernation and relocated to a sunny spot outside the greenhouse.

A guide to overwintering

Before the first frost has been forecast, clear a space in your greenhouse to make way for your more tender plants. This change-over period is the perfect opportunity to give your greenhouse a clean to increase light levels and reduce pests.

- Bring your tender plants into your greenhouse and remove any weeds that may be on the surface of the potting mix, as well as any damaged leaves or stems that may lead to rotting.
- Allow plenty of room around your plants for maximum air circulation, which will help minimize fungal diseases and allow for maximum exposure to light, which is in short supply during the winter.
- Allow your plants to dry out to an extent, with just enough moisture to keep them turgid and to sustain minimal growth. These droughtlike conditions should continue until the early spring.
- With warmer temperatures and increased light levels, your tender plants will start to break into active growth. Increase watering with growth and, from March onward, introduce a weekly seaweed-based fertilizer to help sustain that new shoots.
- When the risk of frosts begins to fall, usually around mid-May, acclimatize plants to outside conditions by using a cold frame, which offers protection at night. As plants become more robust, keep the lid open on milder nights to fully adapt them to the cooler temperatures.

Cut flowers

Greenhouses should work hard for us, and that means not only using them to produce fruits and vegetables, but also taking advantage of the growing conditions they offer to produce cut flowers for our home throughout the year.

One of the biggest issues that gardeners wrestle with when they own a greenhouse is what to do with their structures to make full use of them during the winter months.

There are a number of cut flowers that can be grown in our greenhouses from fall until spring, which takes full advantage of an environment that is protected from the worst of the cold and wet weather, with offerings of much-needed color and floral treats during the early spring. It's also possible to grow summer blooms alongside summer crops, but those extreme temperatures reduce the cast of plants that will cope.

Why grow your own?

There's so much choice when it comes to buying seeds and bulbs compared to flowers from a shop. A packet of seeds that costs the same amount as a cut bunch will produce at least 10 times the number of flowers.

In terms of sustainability, growing your own flowers uses far fewer resources and is much better for the environment than buying them. Importing flowers from around the world using fossil fuels to satisfy our need to have cut flowers outside of the abundance of the summer seems reckless when they're easy to grow in our greenhouses at home. Don't miss out on the pleasure that comes from producing your own cut flowers and the joy you will find in the generosity of these plants. They will fill not just one but probably a few vases in your home every week, and you'll be helping the environment, too, so it's win-win.

Cut flowers from fall to spring

Spring-performing cut flowers will often need to be started off in the fall as bulbs, corms, or seeds. The main driver in growing these flowers in a greenhouse is that they will perform earlier; daffodils, tulips, and sweet peas will all flower sooner than they would outside, and with more perfect blooms. Anemones, ranunculus, and stocks are less inclined to perform well in the garden, as

Anemones grown from corms in the greenhouse can fill a colorful vase in spring.

they dislike the cold and wet, wintery conditions, requiring the protection of a greenhouse to get the best results and long stems. In the case of anemones and ranunculus, they will reward you with huge generosity and plenty of successional flowers, whereas stocks need to be succession-sown in batches every month from January to April and will often produce a cut flower from seed in about 15 weeks.

Anemones (florist types)

Although hardy, these corms detest the wet conditions during the winter and will perform so much better in the protection of a greenhouse. Start off your corms in cell trays in the fall, after soaking them in warm water overnight. As soon as the plants are substantial enough to handle, plant them into beds or large containers, where they will develop and produce flowers in the spring, reaching a height of around 10in (25cm) before slowing down, ready to be replaced by other crops in the early summer. Here are a few to try:

- 'Hollandia'
- 'Mr Fokker'
- 'Mount Everest'

Ranunculus

Gardeners have recently caught on to how wonderful these cut flowers are and how we can easily grow them at home. Like anemones, corms should be soaked overnight and started off in pots in early fall, then planted in the late fall/early winter into beds and containers. Avoid overwatering and hydrate them sparingly when young. They also enjoy cool, bright, drier atmospheres during the winter months. Increase watering and feeding as they grow and temperatures rise. Reaching a height of 12in (30cm), here are a few to try:

- 'Elegance Viola'
- 'Elegance Clementine'
- 'Elegance Rosa'

Planting ranunculus corms

01

Source your corms in the fall and soak them in lukewarm water overnight to hydrate them before planting, which will help with the initial growth.

02

Plant individual corms in a cell tray with a little peat-free potting mix in the base of each cell, then fill to the top with mix. Water to settle the potting mix initially, but avoid overwatering during the winter and early spring. Plant out when large enough to handle and the roots can be seen through the drainage holes at the base of the cells.

01

02

Daffodils

There is no shortage in the colors, forms, and scents that daffodils offer us. I favor the tazetta types, which are heavily scented with a number of flowers on each stem for cutting. Start bulbs off in the fall in pots and beds within your greenhouse, and increase water and seaweed feed as the plants grow and light levels and temperatures increase. Spent bulbs can be planted out in the garden when flowering has finished. Here are a few tazetta types to try:
- 'Avalanche'
- 'Yellow Cheerfulness'
- 'Falconet'

Tulips

I adore growing peony-type tulips as cut flowers; they are shorter than standard garden tulips, so they are more content to grow in containers. The protection of your greenhouse will encourage earlier flowers compared to those in the garden, and the flowers are blemish-free due to the protection from the rain and late frosts. Plant the bulbs at a depth that is three times the height of the bulb in November for flowers in April. It is unlikely that your bulbs will reflower next year due to the severity of cutting the majority of the stem, but it's certainly worth a try, as they may recover and flower in a couple years' time outside. A few of my favorites are:
- 'La Belle Epoque'
- 'Angelique'
- 'Mount Tacoma'

Sweet peas

Growing sweet peas in a greenhouse will encourage earlier blooms and avoids damage to the petals caused by rain and wind. Most sweet peas will produce good cut flowers when sown in the fall and planted in containers or beds in your greenhouse when large enough to handle. Do not allow your sweet peas to dry out, as this will cause stunted growth and shorter stem lengths. You should expect flowers in April and May. Plants can be cleared in time for your summer crops. Here are a few to try as a mixture for long stems and scent:
- 'Matucana'
- 'Gwendoline'
- 'Charlie's Angel'

Stocks

With an unrivaled scent, stocks are joyous to grow and cut for the home. Easy to germinate from seed (see opposite) from the fall and then to overwinter until they flower, they can be sown in batches every month or so for continuous blooms until the early summer, when warmer conditions cause their stem lengths to shorten. Look out for cut-flower varieties, and once plants are in their final pots, apply a nitrogen-based liquid feed to ensure longer stem lengths and avoid premature flowering. Achieving around 2½ft (80cm) in height, the 'Katz' series offers a range of colors and good reliability.

Stocks are easy to grow from seed and have both pretty flowers and wonderful scent.

Sowing stocks

01
Fill a pot with peat-free potting mix and use a seed tamper or the base of another pot to firm and level the surface.

02
Water the potting mix before sowing to avoid disturbing the seeds.

03
Sow seeds over the moist, level surface, nudging them with a wooden skewer to ensure even spacing between each one and avoiding congestion.

04
Cover with a layer of vermiculite and label your seeds.

05
Once germinated, select seedlings to prick out. Light-colored seedlings will often indicate double-flowered plants. Only pick out the lime-colored seedlings for purely double flowers. For a mixed display, prick out all seedlings. Hold the selected seedlings by the seed leaf and carefully tease out the roots with the skewer.

06
Transfer seedlings into cells of peat-free potting mix, gently guiding the roots into the planting hole with the skewer, and water well.

Zinnias enjoy the heat of the greenhouse and bring luminous color to a cut-flower bed.

Cut flowers from summer to fall

Space in the greenhouse can be at a premium during the summer months, making it hard to find room for cut flowers. Plus, the extreme temperatures within a greenhouse in the summer make it less appealing for a number of cut flowers. However, there are some exceptions.

Zinnias and marigolds are very tolerant of warm temperatures and dislike the cooler conditions of the fall, so growing a few in a raised bed in a greenhouse will give you plenty of flowers through those summer months and also offer some attraction for pollinators without taking up too much space. Vigorous, scented-leaf pelargoniums also make great cut flowers, offering wonderful scent and tolerance of warmer temperatures in a greenhouse. To achieve long stems, it is best to keep these plants well fed and watered.

Marigolds

Perfect as companion plants for tomatoes to deter whitefly, but also as a cut flower. Look out for the taller types, which are perfect for cutting. Borders, raised beds, and large containers are the best places to grow these larger marigolds due to their vigor. Here are a few to try:

- 'Burning Embers'
- 'Strawberry Blonde'
- 'Jolly Jester'

Zinnias

Zinnias hail from Mexico and are tolerant of high temperatures, and coupled with the array of gorgeous colors that are available, this makes them a perfect contender for producing cut flowers during the summer in your greenhouse. A raised bed or large container will suit them best to prevent them from drying out (see opposite), which causes stress and reduces their stem length. Zinnias can be sown direct from May to June and will produce flowers until the fall. Although they are a long-established series, the 'Benary's Giant' range is hard to beat, and there are colors to suit all tastes.

Extending vase life

When it comes to cutting your stems, there are a few tricks you can employ to maximize their health and prolong their vase life as much as possible.

- Cut your flowers in the cool of the morning and allow them to spend a day in a bucket of water in a dark place to fully hydrate and condition them.
- When you're ready to arrange your flowers, cut the stems at an angle to maximize the surface area, which allows the stems to absorb more water, and remove any leaves that sit below the water line in the vase. Left on, the leaves will quickly rot and contaminate the water.
- Hygiene is crucial, as clean, regularly refreshed water will drastically prolong your flowers' vase life. If water is allowed to turn green, bacteria can procreate, which will cause the quality to deteriorate and in turn affect your flowers—they will lose condition and need to replaced more regularly. So change your vase water every couple days to keep your flowers as fresh and long-lasting as possible.

Sowing zinnias in a raised bed

01
Prepare the surface of your raised bed to create a level, crumbly surface. Mark out sowing rows with short pieces of bamboo cane placed at 10in (25cm) intervals.

02
Use a board the same length as the raised bed and create shallow drills with your hands along the edge of it, in line with the bamboo canes.

03
Water the drills to make the growing medium tacky and provide moisture underneath the seed to promote germination.

04
Place two or three seeds every 8in (20cm) along each drill.

05
Lightly cover the seed with material from the surface of the raised bed that has accumulated as you created the drills.

Potted bulbs

The protection that your greenhouse provides from the excessive winter wet can be used to great effect in growing a range of bulbs in pots.

Two of the biggest factors for poorly performing bulbs will be rotting off in the winter and being dug up and eaten by rodents. So growing more delicate bulbs in containers and starting them off in your greenhouse will help increase your chances of success.

Bulbs are subject to a seasonal rhythm, meaning that they go through a dormant period when they require no water or food. During this dormant period, when their foliage has dried up, pots can be stored under benching or in a shed, as they require no light and can save a lot of precious space in your greenhouse. Botanically, this group encompasses bulbs, corms, rhizomes, and tubers, but for simplicity's sake, I'll refer to them all as bulbs.

Hardy spring-flowering bulbs

Crocuses, miniature daffodils, and miniature irises can all be grown very successfully in containers within your greenhouse. The extra protection over winter will help keep your blooms in better condition for longer as they come into flower around February and March, and by displaying them on your greenhouse staging, you can appreciate the intricacies of each flower. Dwarf and species tulips or peony types can also be grown successfully in pots, as the protection from the winter wet is extremely beneficial to prevent rot and protect the blooms.

Scented bulbs, such as hyacinths, are also perfect for growing in pots under glass. These can either be taken into the house to flower or left in the greenhouse to fill it with their intoxicating scent. As flower stems develop, they can become top heavy and require support. A few well-placed twigs pushed in around the edge of the pot will provide a framework to support the flowers in a decorative, unimposing way (as above). Given that the weather can still be gray and cold outside in the early spring, sitting at a small table and chairs with a few potted bulbs around you in flower can be a real treat at this time of year.

Hyacinths can be decoratively supported by twigs for a beautiful, scented display.

Potting up spring-flowering bulbs

Spring bulbs are available during the fall in garden centers or online and can be potted up as soon as you get them home. Although dried bulbs are cheaper, with more variety of choice, prepotted bulbs are available from January to April in garden centers and can offer instant impact when potted on into terracotta pots.

01

01
Place a few pieces of broken terracotta over any large drainage holes to prevent potting mix from seeping out of the bottom of the pot. The extra drainage crocks provide is also beneficial, as bulbs dislike being too wet in the winter.

02

02
To further enhance drainage, add a few handfuls of sand to some peat-free potting mix and mix in as you fill the container to around halfway. As a general rule, bulbs should be planted at a depth that is around three times their height.

03

03
For the most impact when in flower, arrange your bulbs across the entirety of the potting mix surface, not quite touching one another. As these bulbs will potentially only be in this pot for a short time, their planting density can be much greater than if they were being planted outside.

04
Cover your bulbs to just below the top of the pot with peat-free potting mix.

05
Add a layer of sand to the surface of the potting mix—this acts as decoration but will also suppress weeds.

06
Label the pot, then water well to settle the potting mix and wash the gravel. Refrain from watering until fresh shoots emerge in the spring. The more foliage your bulbs produce, the more water they can process without rotting, so increase the amount of water you give them as the amount of foliage increases. Your bulbs will flower in a few months' time. After flowering, and when the leaves begin to yellow, reduce the amount of water to encourage your bulbs to go dormant, ready to be potted up again that fall.

04

05

Tip

Repotting your bulbs each fall in fresh compost will give them a boost, although their flowering performance can diminish over time. For a more reliable display, or if you've been disappointed in year two, plant out spent hardy bulbs into your garden and refresh with new bulbs each fall.

06

Keep deadheading daffodils in spring (above), and try tender bulbs like nerines for extra color in summer (right).

Tender bulbs

It is possible to grow a range of tender bulbs in a frost-free greenhouse, and their exotic blooms can bring great joy to your gardening environment. Once you have achieved success with the hardy spring-flowering bulbs and want something a little more challenging, here are a few tender bulbs to try:

- *Achimenes*
- *Eucomis comosa*
- *Gloriosa superba*
- *Haemanthus coccineus*
- *Lachenalia aloides*
- *Nerine sarniensis*
- *Zantedeschia* (calla lily)

Each of these tender bulbs will have different periods of dormancy (when they should be kept dry) and growth (when they need more food and water). Most bulbs require a free-draining soil and are best potted up during their dormant period to avoid unnecessary damage and stress to the plant.

This group of bulbs will flower during the summer and fall, lending some color to your greenhouse, following on from your spring-flowering bulbs. *Eucomis* and *Zantedeschia* will grow successfully outside during the summer. The useful thing about bulbs in a dormant state is that they can be stored under benches, as the absence of leaves means they require no light.

Tip

Fill a large container with daffodil bulbs for cutting and place in a sheltered spot, close to your greenhouse, for a selection of blooms in the early spring the following year. Deadhead after flowering to concentrate energy into the bulb and away from unnecessary seed production.

Plants for summer containers

The majority of summer-flowering plants commonly used in containers will not tolerate frost. Growing these young plants in a greenhouse until the risk of frost has passed will not only protect them, but also encourage growth for a fuller display earlier in summer, delivering instant impact.

The floriferous nature of tender perennials, such as pelargoniums, fuchsias, and heliotropes, make them wonderful additions to containers for summer color. The life cycle of these plants begins with semi-ripe wood cuttings in summer, which are then overwintered in a greenhouse, ready to be planted out when the risk of frost has passed to perform in our gardens. Much-loved varieties of these plants can be kept year on year through that cycle.

How to grow pelargoniums

One of the most iconic and traditional plants that we associate with greenhouses, pelargoniums perform extremely well outside during the summer, attracting far fewer pests than those grown under glass during the warmer months. They come in many forms, and most enjoy a well-lit position and short periods of drought but in turn detest wet, cold soils, especially during the winter. They need lots of air movement and ventilation throughout the year, and it's best to remove any dead or dying leaves during the winter to avoid botrytis and rot.

Potting mix and feeding

Any peat-free potting mix with good drainage will suffice for pelargoniums, although species types will benefit from adding extra sand at a ratio of one part sand to three parts potting mix. Regular potting on and fresh medium in the spring will help keep your pelargoniums actively growing. During spring and summer, feed with a high-potash fertilizer once a week and water more regularly for the best results—although some species pelargoniums will require less water and a monthly feed to avoid excessive lush foliage.

Overwintering

To overwinter pelargoniums in a greenhouse, reduce the plant by half in the fall and place in a frost-free, well-lit, ventilated position. In the spring, when light levels and temperatures increase, plants will begin to grow and can be pruned back a little harder, although regal types do not respond well to hard pruning, which can reduce flowering—better to prune them immediately after flowering.

Most pelargoniums can be easily propagated from semi-ripe wood cuttings (see page 102) in the summer and do not require excessive humidity to root. I achieve good results without a heated propagator or plastic bag around the cuttings, as I find these cause more problems with rot.

Vibrant pelargoniums can be grown from cuttings in the greenhouse over winter in time to give a great display in summer containers.

How to grow fuchsias

Fuchsias are equally at home in a basket or a summer container. Trailing types are more suited to pot edges, whereas upright bush types can provide height in a mixed summer display. Tender fuchsias will not tolerate a frost and tend to be showier than their hardier garden cousins.

Showy fuchsias are happy in containers or hanging baskets, but they can also be trained into a standard.

Potting mix and feeding

Young fuchsias need potting on regularly to produce a healthy, buoyant plant. The cycle of taking cuttings in summer, overwintering in a greenhouse, then planting out after the risk of frost applies to this group. Young plants can be grown in peat-free potting mix and, from February, they can be fed a weekly seaweed fertilizer, switching to a high-potash feed from May to encourage flowering.

Propagation and overwintering

Fuchsias can be grown each year either by taking cuttings or overwintering larger plants. The latter should be reduced by half and watering kept to a minimum until growth restarts in spring. Most fuchsias are easily rooted in summer by semi-ripe wood cuttings. Vine weevil and aphids can be a problem for greenhouse fuchsias in summer, so I prefer to grow them in the garden. An issue with overwintering plants is that you can overwinter pests, too, so taking cuttings and keeping them pest-free will give you a good start the following year and avoid pest build-up in your greenhouse.

Train a fuchsia into a standard

To train a fuchsia into a standard, it's best to start with a rooted cutting, which can be trained up a single cane.

01
Remove any side shoots that develop up the stem until it reaches a height of around 3ft (90cm).

02
Snip off any flower buds until a balanced head has formed to concentrate energy on growth and structure. Continue to remove the shoot tips to promote branching within the head.

01

02

Repot overwintered heliotropes, such as 'White Queen', into fresh potting mix before moving outdoors in summer.

Planting a summer container

The choices of containers for a summer display are vast, and your decision will largely be an aesthetic one based on the space you have available and your preferred material, but the main attribute your container needs is a way for water to drain away. If the drainage hole is large, meaning potting mix may leak out of it, place a layer of broken terracotta pieces over it before adding potting mix.

How to grow heliotropes

Maybe a little less well known than pelargoniums or fuchsias, heliotropes are equally valuable as container plants. These tender perennials come in a range of purples, lilacs, and whites and have the most delicious cherry pie-like scent. Heliotropes can be grown in a greenhouse during the summer, but I find the cooler conditions of the garden or outdoor containers keep plants flowering for longer and help avoid stress due to excessive temperatures within the greenhouse.

Potting mix and feeding

Heliotropes grow happily in peat-free potting mix and should be fed with a seaweed fertilizer from February until May. From May to September, replace this with a high-potash feed. Like many other tender perennials, heliotropes dislike having excessively wet roots in the winter, but as growth begins in the spring and accelerates through the summer, increase watering and feeding to meet the plant's needs. Provide high levels of light and ventilation throughout the year and remove any dead or dying leaves during the winter to avoid pest build-up and botrytis.

Propagation and overwintering

Plants can be overwintered by reducing their size by half before the risk of frosts, potting them up, and bringing them into a frost-free greenhouse. When growth begins in spring, plants can be cut back to a lower, healthy shoot to regenerate for the summer. Heliotropes are easily propagated by semi-ripe wood cuttings (see page 102), which can be taken in the summer and overwintered in a greenhouse.

A summer display of *Iresine lindenii*, *Pelargonium* 'Orangeade', and *Calibrachoa* 'Cabaret Deep Blue'.

Instructions

01
Fill your container close to the top with peat-free potting mix and arrange your plants within the container to the style of your choice without planting them. This is your opportunity to play around with different combinations and make sure that you're happy with the final display before you commit to your design by planting.

02
Once you're happy with your arrangement, plant your young plants into the potting mix just below their current planting depth, beginning with your focal plant and working outward from there to the edges.

03
Water thoroughly, and after a few weeks, begin a supplementary routine of a high-potash feed until the first frosts.

01

02

03

Plants for containers

A handy design principle to follow when planting up containers is to use a "thriller" plant as the central focal point, a "filler" to give the display fullness, and a "spiller" to trail over the edge. Bear this in mind when choosing your plants.

Thrillers
Impatiens New Guinea Group
Salvia farinacea
Upright fuchsia
Upright pelargonium

Fillers
Ageratum
Antirrhinum
Argyranthemum
Begonia
Bush petunia
Heliotrope
Marigold
Nemesia
Osteospermum

Spillers
Bacopa
Calibrachoa (million bells)
Dichondra argentea 'Silver Falls'
Lobelia
Lotus berthelotii
Trailing fuchsia
Trailing pelargonium
Trailing petunia
Trailing verbena

Bursting with color, this hanging display shows off trailing "spiller" plants—such as lobelia, calibrachoa, bacopa, and *Lotus berthelotii*—to their best advantage.

Planting a hanging basket

Hanging baskets provide a riot of color at height in the summer—a front door adorned with a colorful basket is a wonderful sight. I'm a bit of a sucker for the traditional hanging basket full of pelargoniums, fuchsias, heliotropes, and petunias, but you can let your imagination run wild and free here. Salad plants, strawberries, herbs, tomatoes, or even succulents can all look wonderful in a basket and can be hung at an accessible height. The bigger the basket, the better, because the larger volume of growing medium will retain more moisture and dry out less frequently.

A great benefit of owning a greenhouse is that we can plant up our baskets as soon as plants are available online and in garden centers, taking advantage of a wider variety that are less expensive. This allows our hanging baskets time to grow in protected, warmer conditions before we position them outside toward the end of May, when the risk of frost is greatly reduced, giving us instant impact. Because these young plants will grow quickly, keep them well watered while under glass, but avoid completely saturating the potting mix until the plants have established.

What you'll need

Hanging basket (wire, woven wicker, or plastic)
There are lots of different types of baskets available. The benefit of using a wire basket is that you can insert trailing plants throughout, giving you a much fuller effect compared to a solid basket.

Liner or moss Premade liners are available in different sizes, often with precut holes. Using sphagnum moss for lining is becoming a little contentious, so make sure you're getting your moss from a sustainable source if using.

Circle of plastic Take an old mulch bag and cut a circle to cover the base of the basket to hold that little bit of moisture in a reservoir.

Peat-free potting mix Any multipurpose, peat-free potting mix will be sufficient.

Seaweed and tomato fertilizer Water daily through the summer and feed at least once a week. Use seaweed fertilizer until you are content that the plants have filled in and are ready to start producing lots of flowers. At that point, switch to a tomato feed, which will promote flowers instead of foliar growth.

Deadheading

Regular removal of spent flowers, or deadheading, will encourage large numbers of new flower buds to form, especially if coupled with a feeding routine. If your plants are left alone and allowed to produce seed, the signals within the plants are sending the message that its job is done and flowers are no longer required.

Instructions

01
Sit the basket inside a terracotta pot and line the inside of the basket with a premade liner, or add a generous layer of moss over the bottom third of the basket. Add your reusable plastic circle at the base of the basket, inside the liner.

02
If using a premade liner, create holes in the side of it (if not precut) in the top two-thirds of the basket using scissors. Holes any lower may allow potting mix to escape when the roots haven't filled the basket. Also make one hole in the plastic circle.

03
Add potting mix to the bottom third of the basket to the level of the cut holes in the liner or moss.

04
Feed in the root balls of your trailing "spiller" plants from the outside, gently threading them through in an all-around effect. Add potting mix to cover the root balls of the plants within the sides, adding more potting mix to within a few centimeters or inches of the top of the liner or continuing to moss the rest of the basket as a liner before you add the remaining potting mix.

05
Add your "thriller" plants to the center of the basket as a focal point, then your cushion "filler" plants around the edge and fill potting mix around them.

06
Water well, including a seaweed fertilizer, and use a rose attachment on the watering can to settle the potting mix around the plants without causing too much disturbance. Hang your basket from the roof of your greenhouse where you choose until the risk of frost has passed.

01 02 03 04 05 06

The greenhouse year

Seed-sowing calendar

Over the years, I have honed a seed-sowing schedule to produce vegetables, cut flowers, and a variety of plants for greenhouses that works well and helps curb the sunshine-induced enthusiasm to sow everything at once.

Ultimately, we're looking to propagate a healthy plant from seed, which has begun to root out of the drainage holes at the base of the pot, as these plants will establish quickly and successfully. Sow too early and roots become congested (there's only so much time and space to continually pot on) and your plants won't reach their full potential.

Successional sowing

Successional sowing is an activity or discipline that can be lost in the intensity of greenhouse growing in the spring and summer. Taking time to plan successional sowing of fast-growing crops, such as spring onions, salad leaves, and herbs–and sticking to that plan–will ensure that you're regularly cropping throughout the summer, avoiding a boom-or-bust approach. Below are just a few seeds to sow successionally in your greenhouse, at four-week intervals:

- Carrots
- Bush green beans
- Peas
- Spinach
- Arugula
- Cilantro
- Lettuce
- Dill
- Beets
- Spring onions
- Salad leaves

Salad leaves can be sown into covered beds or containers.

Calendulas flower profusely, cut well, and even have edible petals.

Sowing calendar: ornamentals

January
Sweet pea
Ammi majus (false bishop's weed)
Daucus carota (wild carrot)
Scabiosa atropurpurea (sweet scabious)
Petunia

February
Antirrhinum (snapdragons)
Cobaea scandens (cup and saucer vine)
Papaver somniferum
Heliophila longifolia
Schizanthus
Stocks
Calibrachoa

March
Dahlia
Cerinthe major 'Purpurascens'
Marigolds
Amaranthus (can be grown as an edible or ornamental)
Carthamus tinctorius
Ricinus
Tithonia
Eschscholzia
Statice
Ipomea
Calendula (flowers are edible and ornamental)

April
Cleome
Cosmos
Rudbeckia
Xerochrysum bracteatum
Sunflower
Indigo

May
Callistephus
Ornamental gourd
Zinnia

June
Alstroemeria
Erigeron

July / August
Wallflowers
Bellis
Sweet William
Foxgloves
Icelandic poppies
Forget-me-not

September
Nigella
Calendula (flowers are edible and ornamental)

Sowing calendar: edibles

January
Spinach (perpetual types)
Parsley
Onion
Fava bean
Lemongrass

February
Lettuce
Spinach (summer types)
Chilies
Bell pepper

March
Borage
Eggplant
Lettuce
Celery root
Tomato
Cabbage (fall types)
Brussels sprouts
Amaranthus (can be grown as an edible or ornamental)
Calendula (flowers are edible and ornamental)

April
Leek
Cucumber
Lettuce
Kalette
Kale
Gherkin
Luffa cylindrica
Beets
Melon

May
Zucchini
Marrow
Lettuce
Pole bean
Runner bean
Sweet corn
Parsnip
Winter squash
Pumpkin

June
Lettuce
Chard
Beets
Purple sprouting broccoli
Fennel

July / August
Chicory
Lettuce

September
Beets (for winter storage)
Spring cabbage

A season of edibles all grown from seed might include (clockwise from top left) lemongrass, peppers, tomatoes, melons, and loofahs.

The greenhouse year: mid- to late winter

Don't worry that your plants aren't growing a lot during this time of year. Overwatering and cold drafts are the biggest issues in a greenhouse full of tender plants, so keep your environment insulated and water sparingly for successful "growing." We are managing our plants in a dormantlike state by keeping them ticking along with minimal growth.

January

- Start seed sowing of hardy crops, such as parsley, fava beans, and sweet peas (see page 200).
- Plant parsley either grown from seed or using plants bought from a supermarket.
- Pot on tender perennials and pinch back tips to encourage branched growth and remove any aphids that may congregate on the soft growth.
- Use hazel twigs to stake early flowering bulbs as they emerge, such as cape cowslips (*Lachenalia aloides*) and hyacinths.
- Chit potatoes.

February

- Start feeding regime with a liquid seaweed fertilizer for most crops for strong root development and healthy growth.
- Start sweet potatoes from a tuber, ginger from a root, and lemongrass from seed and from stems in a heated propagator (see pages 164, 172, and 168).
- Increase the amount of water for growing bulbs.
- Research biological-control providers and contact them to discuss the crops that you'll be growing and a schedule for deliveries of predators.
- Sow hardy and half-hardy annuals and prick out seedlings when the true set (second pair) of leaves appear, moving trays from warmer to cooler environments as plants grow to harden off.
- Sow chili and pepper seeds.
- Keep ranunculus and anemones moist. Spray once a week with a mixture to prevent powdery mildew (see page 123). Continue this throughout March and April.
- Use SB Plant Invigorator spray weekly to prevent aphid and other sap-sucking pests from building up.
- Chit potatoes.

Midwinter tasks include (clockwise from top left): sowing fava beans; chitting seed potatoes; sowing chili and pepper seeds; sprouting sweet potato tubers.

CHILLI
'EARLY CAYENNE'
22/02

The greenhouse year: early to mid-spring

The extra warmth and protection that a greenhouse provides during the early spring enables us to encourage plants and seeds into growth earlier than we would if they were exposed to the outdoor climate. Young plants can be started from seed and, although tentative to begin with, can be watered and fed as their growth accelerates.

March

- Pollinate nectarines, peaches, and apricots that are growing under glass with a small, soft paintbrush.
- Take chrysanthemum and dahlia cuttings when fresh growth emerges.
- Continue to sow and grow on hardy and half-hardy annuals.
- At the first signs of growth, divide and pot up tuberous begonias into terracotta pots. Start watering as growth emerges but lightly to begin with, increasing the amount as the plant grows.
- Repot overwintered fuchsias, pelargoniums, and heliotropes.
- Pot on young plants as they begin to show roots through the base of the pot.
- Use insecticidal soap spray weekly to prevent aphid and other sap-sucking pests from building up.
- Plant out your sweet peas, hardy annuals, and fava beans.
- Create a tunnel cloche to protect early lettuce (see page 32).
- Make a batch of nettle fertilizer when growth starts (see page 82).

Plant growth gets going in spring. Give it a boost by making your own nettle fertilizer and applying when you water.

Water spring bulbs as they grow and remove spent flower heads once they go over.

April

- Pot on young plants as they begin to show roots through the base of their container. Transfer to a pot no bigger than twice the size of the existing pot (see page 96).
- Move tender perennials to cold frames to harden them off (see page 25).
- Thin apricots, nectarines, and peaches to encourage larger fruits.
- Check grapevines for mildew and spray if necessary with a preventative mixture (see page 123). Tie in and prune.
- Use insecticidal soap spray weekly to prevent aphid and other sap-sucking pests from building up.
- Continue with seaweed feeding regime.
- Pot up or plant out stocks into their final flowering position and stake with split canes.
- As daffodils and hyacinths come to the end of their flowering season, remove the spent flowers and feed once a week with a high-potash fertilizer until mid-May, then allow to die back and dry out.
- Pot up lilies into terracotta pots for patio displays.
- At the first signs of growth, start to pot up kohlerias and achimenes.
- Paint the outside of greenhouses with shading paint or hang shade netting to reduce light intensity and temperatures.
- Move cannas and bananas outdoors in order to acclimatize them to cooler temperatures.
- Plant up hanging baskets and keep them frost-free while temperatures remain low.

Fava beans grown from seed in the greenhouse from January will be ready to plant out in rows in March.

The greenhouse year: late spring to early summer

With higher temperatures and light levels, late spring marks a transitional time in our greenhouses where we prepare for the summer bounty by proactively growing our young plants through potting on. Plants that are not suited to the warmer environment under glass make way for supports and containers full of tomatoes, cucumbers, eggplants, peppers, and melons.

May

- Check that ties on all trained fruit are not causing constriction; replace them and tie more loosely where required.
- Continue with feeding regime of a weekly seaweed-based fertilizer to develop stems and strong growth, ready to support fruit and flowers.
- Pot up chilies, peppers, tomatoes, cucumbers, and eggplants into their final pots, grow bags, and beds.
- Move mints outside to prevent mildew and pests.
- Use insecticidal soap spray weekly to prevent aphid and other sap-sucking pests from building up.
- Start introducing biological controls.
- Remove sweet potato slips and root in water. Pot up when a reasonable amount of root has grown.
- Make a batch of comfrey fertilizer (see page 82).
- Plant summer containers.

June

- Turn off greenhouse heating when risk of frosts has passed.
- Plant out dahlias and chrysanthemums.
- Remove side shoots from cordon tomatoes and cucumbers (aside from lunchbox types).
- Continue with feeding regime, switching to a potash-based fertilizer when plants are established.
- Tie in melon side shoots to produce fruit.
- Support tomatoes, cucumbers, and peppers with string or canes.

Jobs for these months include (clockwise from top left): making comfrey fertilizer; planting out dahlias; supporting cordon tomatoes and other climbing fruits and vegetables with string or canes; moving mint outside to prevent pests and diseases.

The greenhouse year: mid- to late summer

Plants are reaching their peak growth now, and their demands for water and food are at their greatest. Keep that husbandry going to get the best from your plants, including the removal of dead or dying leaves to prevent disease. It's not all about work; there's lots of harvesting and eating, too.

July

• Keep feeding plants on a regular basis–they're in full growth and will need it.
• Apply a soap- or oil-based spray weekly to the soft growth at the top of plants to prevent pests and disease.
• Repot lachenalias and nerines and water once a week.
•Take cuttings of tender perennials, such as fuchsias, pelargoniums, and heliotrope.
• Start sowing biennial seeds, such as foxgloves, sweet Williams, poppies, and honesty.
• Harvest and prune nectarines and peaches. Remove fruited wood to replace with new growth.
• Remove side shoots from tomatoes while training.
• Apply biological controls where necessary.
• Open vents and doors during the day (see page 44) and damp down (see page 114) around humidity-loving plants, such as cucumbers, melons, and eggplants.
• Make sure shading levels are correct (see page 66). If not, apply another coat of shading paint or increase the amount of glass that is covered by shading fabric.

August

• Remove the lower leaves of eggplants, tomatoes, and cucumbers as they deteriorate to prevent disease and increase airflow.
• Pick tomatoes, chilies, and peppers regularly to encourage more fruits.
• Continue to feed plants on a regular basis.
• Deadhead flowering plants, such as pelargoniums.
• Harvest cut flowers, such as zinnias.
• Apply a soap- or oil-based spray weekly to the soft growth at the top of plants to prevent pests and disease.
• Continue to remove side shoots from tomatoes while training.
• Continue to apply biological controls where and when necessary.
• Continue to open vents and doors during the day (see page 44) and damp down (see page 114) around humidity-loving plants, such as cucumbers, melons, and eggplants.
• Check that ties on all trained fruit are not causing any constriction.

Jobs for summer include (clockwise from top left): picking tomatoes; harvesting cut flowers, such as zinnias; deadheading pelargoniums.

The greenhouse year: early to mid-fall

You'll notice that growth and the general vibrancy of the plants in your greenhouse are starting to fade as those cooler evenings and lower light levels arrive. It's important to encourage a healthy environment in the greenhouse at this time, as well as reduce watering and feeding. This is also the time to prepare for stormy weather later in the season.

September

- Continue to remove lower leaves of eggplants, tomatoes, and cucumbers as they deteriorate to prevent disease and increase airflow.
- Continue to pick tomatoes, chilies, and peppers regularly to encourage more fruits.
- Continue to feed plants on a regular basis.
- Continue to apply a soap- or oil-based spray weekly to the soft growth at the top of plants to prevent pests and disease.
- Continue to apply biological controls where and when necessary.
- Keep paths weed- and algae-free.
- Remove greenhouse shading (see page 66) toward the end of the month as light levels drop.
- Reduce ventilation (see page 44) and humidity (see page 114) as temperatures cool.
- Remove any tired or damaged foliage to prevent disease and increase airflow.
- Check any heaters to ensure that they are in good working order.
- Monitor weather forecasts and bring in plants for overwintering before any frosts.
- Bring in citrus, peaches, and apricot trees.

October

- Bring in succulents to protect them from heavy rain and temperatures below 41°F (5°C).
- Introduce heating when colder weather comes in. Preventing the temperature from dropping below freezing will keep overwintering tender plants in a content, slightly dormant state.
- Reduce watering. It's easy to revive a dry plant but almost impossible to resurrect a cold, sodden one.
- Start sowing winter salads, such as mustards, winter lettuce, and perpetual spinach (see page 136).
- Throw out parent plants of cuttings when rooted to maximize space.
- Withhold water to dry off kohlerias and begonias before the frosts, then store in a frost-free place.
- Lift and repot tropical and tender perennials, such as dahlias, cannas, musa, and ensete, as new signs of life appear. Bring into the greenhouse to protect from winter weather before planting out in spring.
- Start propagating next year's cut flowers: sow stocks; plant ranunculus tubers and anemone corms in cell trays. Plant up when large enough to handle.
- Make nettle fertilizer (see page 82) for spring use.
- Wash plant pots and trays in warm, soapy water.
- Wash and treat woodwork to preserve it for winter.

Prepare the greenhouse for storms

In early fall, before the more turbulent weather arrives, make sure your greenhouse is structurally sound to avoid the risk of damage from the elements. Here are a few things to check:

- Inspect the outside of your greenhouse for any loose fixings or panes of glass that may have slipped, and check that vents and doors are aligned and sit securely within their runners.
- Make sure that all vents and doors are closed and well secured. If you have automatic vents, it may be worth disconnecting them to prevent them from opening and catching the wind. A secure, closed greenhouse will be resistant to the wind.
- Replace any broken or missing panes of glass. If this is not possible before the bad weather arrives, cover the hole with a sheet of plastic or an old blanket and secure to prevent wind damage.
- Ensure the greenhouse is well anchored to its base. Bags of compost or sandbags can be used to anchor any flanges.
- Secure any external hazards that may blow into your greenhouse, such as furniture or trampolines.

Fall jobs include planting anemone corms in cell trays (above left) and planting them out when large enough (above).

The greenhouse year: late fall to early winter

During late fall, we sense a shift in the weather and the way our plants react. Cooler evening temperatures and lower light levels cause plant growth to slow down, and excessive moisture in the greenhouse environment becomes problematic. This seasonal shift presents an opportunity to refresh and bring on a whole new host of plants to inhabit your greenhouse during the winter.

November

- Order seeds to have access to the best range before lines sell out.
- Plant strawberry hanging baskets and hang inside your greenhouse for an earlier crop.
- Sow sweet peas in root trainers.
- Rehouse chrysanthemums in a frost-free greenhouse with good light levels. The added protection will bring plants into growth in the new year, from which cuttings can be taken when shoots are long enough.
- Lift and divide mint for winter harvest.
- Remove vine and fig foliage. Prune vines back to two nodes.
- Pot up spring bulbs, such as hyacinths, amaryllis, daffodils, irises, and tulips, into terracotta pots or in raised beds for cut flowers.
- Harvest sweet potatoes and encourage slips for next year (see page 164).
- Move fuchsias under glass and keep roots dry.
- Clean your greenhouse and oil mechanisms.
- Keep paths weed- and algae-free.
- Add a layer of bubble-wrap insulation inside the greenhouse to protect plants from extreme cold.

December

- Retie in all trained fruit with fresh ties for health to reduce pest levels and to avoid constriction.
- Cut back canna foliage (which will begin to brown and die back if not already cut down when lifted earlier in the fall) to encourage fresh growth when temperatures rise. Winter-damaged foliage on most tropical plants can be removed to prevent pests from building up and to prepare for new shoots in the spring.
- Harden off and plant more tender bulbs and corms, such as anemones and ranunculus, transitioning from a heated environment to cooler conditions where they are to flower. Keep moist. Spray once a week with a mixture to prevent powdery mildew (see page 123).
- Lift greenhouse blinds to increase light transmission.
- Clean your greenhouse to remove grime, cool the glass, and increase light levels. Oil any moving mechanisms, such as vents and doors.

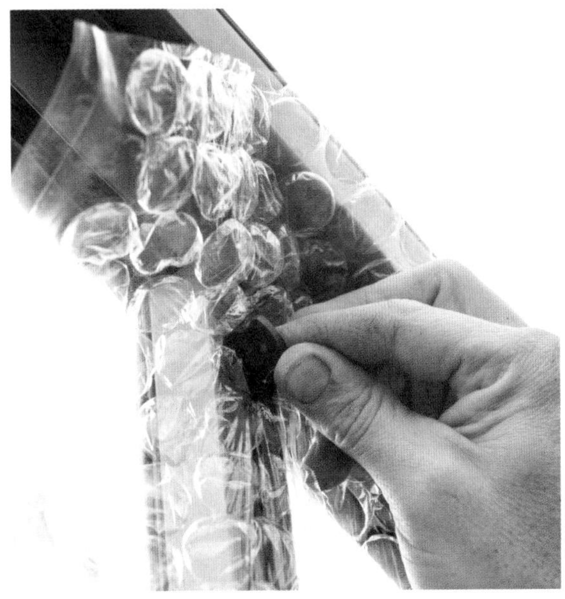

Jobs for late fall include (clockwise from top left): planting spring bulbs and corms; sowing sweet peas in root trainers; insulating the greenhouse with bubble wrap; lifting blinds to increase light.

Index

Page numbers in *italics* refer to illustrations

D

E

Picture credits

The publisher would like to thank the following for their kind permission to reproduce their photographs:

(Key: a-above; b-below/bottom; c-center; f-far; l-left; r-right; t-top)

13 GAP Photos: Elke Borkowski (cr); Robert Mabic (br). **14 Bridgeman Images. 15 Getty Images:** Hulton Archive. **18 Alamy Stock Photo:** Nick Maslen. **19 Alamy Stock Photo:** Bailey-Cooper Photography. **80 Alamy Stock Photo:** Jeanette Teare Garden Images. **127 Alamy Stock Photo:** Alexandre Patchine (t). **Getty Images/iStock:** Tunatura (b). **189 Getty Images/iStock:** Olena Lialina (tr)

Author's acknowledgments

Growing plants in a greenhouse can be as intense or sedate as you choose, depending on your ambition and time. When it comes to writing a book about as many horticultural possibilities as you can fit under one roof, the scales tip toward the more demanding side. I would still be mulling over the plans and instructions for the greenhouse if it weren't for the support of my wife, Clare, and my in-laws, Reg and Anne. Many minor family disagreements came and went during the build, but all passed with a cup of tea and the mantra that tomorrow was another day.

I was incredibly lucky to be partnered with Jason Ingram for the photography—his eye and flair are second to none, and he's captured the seasonality of the greenhouse year perfectly. Alastair, our editor, was always encouraging and helped us stay on the straight and narrow. Despite Perry, my young labrador, being distinctly suspicious of him to begin with, eventually they ended up great friends. Thanks also to Holly, Glenda, Jordan, Ruth, and the rest of the DK team who worked on the book.

The Greenhouse People proved to be incredibly helpful and were generous in their delivery of the 18-foot (5.5-m) Robinsons Rosette model, along with the fixtures and fittings. Access Garden Products were also very kind in their support and delivery of the lean-to greenhouse, which turned out to be an incredibly productive smaller space.

Publisher's acknowledgments

DK would like to thank Kathy Steer for proofreading, Vanessa Bird for indexing, and Myriam Meguarbi for picture research.

Editorial Manager Ruth O'Rourke
Senior Editor Alastair Laing
Senior US Editor Kayla Dugger
Executive US Editor Lori Cates Hand
Senior Designer Glenda Fisher
Project Art Editor Jordan Lambley
Design Assistant Izzy Poulson
Senior Production Editor Tony Phipps
Senior Production Controller Samantha Cross
Jacket Designer Jordan Lambley
Publishing Assistant Emily Cannings
Art Director Maxine Pedliham

Editorial Holly Kyte
Design Geoff Borin, Christine Keilty
Photography Jason Ingram
Illustration Paohan Chen, Dan Crisp

First American Edition, 2025
Published in the United States by DK Publishing,
a division of Penguin Random House LLC
1745 Broadway, 20th Floor, New York, NY 10019

25 26 27 28 29 10 9 8 7 6 5 4 3 2 1
001–341191–Mar/2025

Published in Great Britain by Dorling Kindersley Limited

A catalog record for this book is available from the Library of Congress.
ISBN 978-0-5939-5945-9

Printed and bound in China

www.dk.com

This book was made with Forest Stewardship Council™ certified paper—one small step in DK's commitment to a sustainable future.
Learn more at www.dk.com/uk/information/sustainability

About the author

I began my career at the RHS Garden Wisley, learning my craft and progressing to management level by my late twenties. I soon felt a need to develop my own style and take on a garden where I could channel my creativity and indulge in all aspects of horticulture, from orchards to mixed borders and, most importantly, greenhouses. I took up the post of head gardener at Parham House & Gardens in West Sussex for 10 years, and then in May 2019, I moved on to my current role as head gardener at West Dean Gardens, which has 13 large Victorian glasshouses containing an array of ornamental plants and edible crops, grown with sustainable and environmentally friendly methods.

I am also a senior judge at the RHS Chelsea Flower Show and a broadcaster, and I regularly write for *BBC Gardeners' World* magazine, *Which? Gardening*, and the *Daily Telegraph* on Saturday. This is my first book, and I hope you enjoy reading it, giving a go to some of the mini-projects, and growing some of the plants as much as I've enjoyed sharing this experience with you.